HEAL YOUR MIND
HEAL YOUR LIFE

A Mindset Mastery Roadmap to Release Fear
Awaken to Your Highest Self
and Create a Powerful Life

by Monica Dubay

HEAL YOUR MIND
HEAL YOUR LIFE

A Mindset Mastery Roadmap to Release Fear
Awaken to Your Highest Self
and Create a Powerful Life

by Monica Dubay

"Your holiness reverses all the laws of the world. It is
beyond every restriction of time, space, distance and
limits of any kind."

A Course in Miracles

ENDORSEMENTS

In her book," Heal Your Mind, Heal Your Life", Monica Dubay shares her journey from living at the effect of her circumstances to awakening to her own power and living a life of Transformation. She shares in such a way that she actually develops and delivers a pathway of discovery for each of her readers. As I read her book, I am present to the possibility of living a created life that is available to each of us!

This woman is heroic! She is living a life of grace and ease and is offering each of us the opportunity to create the same.

SHERRY LUCKI
Principal, ABTSolutions, iMED and HCS Therapy
ABTSolutions.com | gotoimed.com | hcstherapy.com

I have been working with Monica Dubay for over a year, and every time we talk it is an amazing experience. She is extremely intuitive, loving, and always compassionate. I have learned to trust her like no other person with my deepest fears and thoughts, allowing her to help me transform them to the light and positive in a powerful way.

Monica's book is like having a long, uplifting conversation about how you can transform and move beyond heartbreak, divorce, loss of custody, and even abuse and create a powerful life. I have experienced her wisdom and grace in my life and wish it upon you as well. Embrace her wise words into your consciousness…let your life be transformed.

CLAUDIA BROWN
Strategic Business Success Coach | Anael Consulting, LLC
AnaelBusinessStrategies.com | anaelconsultingllc.com

If you are unsure of your life's purpose or feel you have strayed from it, or you just feel lost and overwhelmed, Monica can help. She's an empath, a teacher, and a healer. She is a beacon of Love and Light that can strengthen your inner sense of self so you can move away from your distress, darkness or doubt, and move forward with more certainty and confidence. She sounds out examples of thoughts that produce pure and positive energy and sifts out those that are part of damaging or self-destructive patterns.

Her visualizations, spiritual and emotional clearing exercises, and thought-provoking questioning tools provide practical, every-day guidance you can rely on again and again to restore and maintain meaning to your actions and efforts. You'll quickly want to add this book to your collection of favorites.

SHARON McCOLLICK
Principal Business Architect / Strategist | Strong Point Strategy, LLC| strongpointstrategy.com

Within the first few pages, I have already experienced a moment of eureka or "ah-ha"! That is what it is to read Monica's book.

While it is literature, it resembles more a dialogue between Monica and your Higher Self. Her wisdom, compassion, and liveliness is felt through her words, allowing for reflection and reception. As your journey through her book, during and afterwards, you can expect lucidity, touching upon every aspect of your life. Whether it be over a resonating belief, originating from your childhood, or an inability to let something or someone go. Her book shows you not only what causes your suffering, but also the beginnings of how to understand it, and release it, so that you can be who you really are.

I have collaborated with and been counseled by Monica. Her Back to Basics program has completely transformed my life. Having tried different holistic therapies, and attended different workshops, they provided tools to experience your surroundings - to survive. But none of them provided tools to experience yourself – to live, to release learned beliefs, to release a learned self. Monica's program gives a structured guidance for this and her book can be viewed as an introduction.

JADE DEANE

Published by
Monica Dubay Publications
Publisher Monica Dubay's email: healyourmindnow@gmail.com

ISBN: 978-0-578-78873-9 Paperback

Disclaimer

The views expressed are those of the author and do not reflect the official policy or position of the publisher or Monica Dubay Publications. This publication is designed to provide accurate and authoritative information regarding the subject matter covered. It is sold with the understanding that the publisher is not engaged in rendering legal, accounting, clinical or other professional advice. If legal advice or other expert assistance is required, the services of a competent professional should be sought. The opinions expressed by the authors in this book are not endorsed by Monica Dubay Publications, and are the sole responsibility of the author rendering the opinion.

DEDICATION

I dedicate this book to my two sons,
Christopher and Samuel, who always teach
me the meaning of unconditional love.

ACKNOWLEDGEMENTS

There are so many people in my life who supported me and encouraged me to complete this book after years of writing and rewriting. My dearest friends, Marielle School, Claudia Brown, Nancy Fitzgerald, Robin Ann Reid, and Melanie Pledger. Their love has been instrumental to my well-being.

My parents, whose love and dedication to family is a guiding light throughout my life. My siblings and their families who are always there for me and have brought me so much joy.

To Lisa Natoli and Bill Free, who always inspire me to be bold.

Jackie Morey, who encouraged me and patiently guided me through the process of self-publishing. Linda Joy for publishing my stories and giving me the courage to keep writing.

The Master Teacher, whose incredible presence lit up my mind with love for all of humanity.

Byron Katie, for her work and guiding light.

My clients who have taught me so much about healing, courage and trust.

Countless friends who continue to have conversations that enlighten and heal. I so appreciate you!

All the spiritual support, whose love is palpable and ever-present.

The millions who are involved with bringing *A Course in Miracles* into the world, especially those at Endeavor Academy for their service and love.

All the leaders on the planet today who are dedicated to the evolution of humanity, including everyone at Landmark Worldwide, especially Sherry Lucki for mentoring me and helping me stand in my power and leadership.

TABLE OF CONTENTS

FOREWORD

Purpose and Focus

The purpose of this book is to help you discover who you are.

Spiritual mastery is the purpose of my life.

Here's how to tell if you should read this book:

Do you want to discover your life purpose?

Do you long for a better connection to your real Self?

Do you desire to master your mind and take better care of yourself and your family?

Do you aspire to have an impact?

Do you yearn for a life that reflects who you really are and that solves a problem you care about?

Do you want to learn to release fear, self-doubt, and guilt?

Do you desire for more peace and clarity for your life?

If you answered yes to any of these questions, keep reading. But be prepared to be confronted and, if you allow, ultimately released from your constructed self-identity.

I want only happiness and freedom from fear and self-doubt – for you.

Self-realization creates power – the power that comes from love, the Source of all life.

The questions at the end of each chapter are designed to challenge you to go within and have breakthroughs in consciousness.

The fact is that you have all power and freedom right now. It's already who you are.

Yet perhaps these are just words. And just words won't cut it.

Experience is key.

My Journey

I have spent more than three decades focusing on mind training and teaching *A Course in Miracles*. I have taught energy healing and a broad range of methods of emotional release that lead to self-realization. I started writing this book about four years ago and it has evolved into what you now hold.

Where it all began:

I was healed of depression and anxiety using the mind training of *A Course in Miracles* when I was 30. Ten years later, I went to a dedicated environment for healing the mind with a Master Teacher who was fully enlightened. Being in the presence of such a Master, was indeed a rare privilege and greatly altered my life path.

I have traveled and taught *A Course in Miracles* in Europe, South America and Australia and the U.S. My experience of transformation over these years and teaching the principles inspired me to teach others the power of the mind to transform their lives.

I have dedicated my life to healing the mind and have explored many spiritual teachings and have gleaned what has helped me and want to share from my experience in the hopes that it will save you time and needless struggle.

My Message

You are an infinite being with infinite potential to create the life you want.

I believe the ultimate purpose in life is to know who we are, why we are here and how we can evolve our species into a new enlightened humanity.

We can only do this if we embrace the reality of love and joy that resides within us, in spite of our fear or conditioning from the past.

INTRODUCTION

My spiritual gift is healing the mind, helping people shift their beliefs and connect to their Real Self. It's always available if you know how to connect.

After spending 12 years in a dedicated spiritual teaching environment, similar to an ashram, I moved back to the East Coast to be nearer my grown boys and my family and I started a healing/coaching program called *Heal Your Mind Heal Your Life*.

I became a healer for other healers and coaches, people who want to make a difference. I quickly became aware that people are suffering with the same ideas. We all have similar issues and beliefs and we can release them easily if we know how. I began to offer courses and workshops in healing the mind and participants got results.

What's the message of this book?

The mind is the key to mastering your life.

You have never not been your Real Self. No matter what, you can't lose your Self. You can't die. You can't lose what you love. Ever.

Even though we experience loss here, there isn't any such thing in the grand scheme of things because life is eternal. But you may not believe that and that's fine. It's an experience, not a theory or set of beliefs, and your beliefs won't alter the fact that God is.

YOU are already the whole, complete Self that God created.

You may have been telling yourself stories about how your life is difficult, perplexing, often impossible and frustratingly mysterious and ultimately, pointless.

I know.

I get it.

I found the secret to how to live, how to trust my inner voice, how to defy what everyone has told me, and even what I have been taught to believe. I chose to open up to constant self-awareness and release the past by embracing my own journey.

I learned to let go of what I knew, entertain a completely new way of thinking, being and acting, so that I could be free.

The job of awakening, and it does require work, dedication, and perseverance, feels never-ending.

Because it is.

Life is eternal after all, and has no edges, no end, no arrival point. Time isn't even sequencing. There is only now. We are constantly challenged to go one step further. Face one more fear. Defy one more belief. Embrace one more idea that changes how you thought a moment ago.

It's an adventure into consciousness.

And it's a wild ride.

Where Do Our Beliefs Come From?

Our belief system is formed around the events we experienced long ago, not just in this lifetime, but probably many, many others. Those experiences were very real. Yet, the past is over. Our deepest memories, are all over and gone.

So why do they still come into our mind and wreak havoc in our life?

Our mind holds onto stories within memory and we believe they are true. We so want them to be real, and they actually define who we are. We keep our stories alive because we are identified by them, even when they cause deep pain and suffering.

Once we understand how we can unhinge ourselves from our memories, and notice them, but not buy into them, we can become free.

Our power lies in our ability to choose what we want to believe.

It's A Serious Problem

Most of us human beings really don't change until we are forced to. Perhaps something unexpected happens, and we finally start to question what is really going on. We need to make sense of these powerful events, yet the harder we try to figure it out on our own the harder it gets.

Although we like our stories, they never really bring us satisfaction. We notice that we keep repeating the same thing with different characters in our life and we are frustrated and often shocked by that realization. "Not that again? I thought I'd healed that" is a complaint I often hear.

But that's just how your brain works. It remembers the past and is always sifting through memories to find out how to respond to events that happen now. Then we make up a future that is not there, and we use our energy to ward off those thoughts too, even though they have no reality.

Denial plays a very big part in the drama we call our lives. We aren't ready to see what would rock our world and turn it upside down when we don't get what we think we want. Sometimes, there's a really good reason to deny what we don't want to face, because it may be too painful to remember.

Yet, we have to admit finally, that we do have power and when we actually choose to exercise it and find the way to awaken from the past, no matter how traumatic it was, we are surprised to find one simple law that holds true no matter what.

Cause And Effect – It's The Law

Thoughts create perception. There is no separation between cause and effect.

The common denominator of my life is me. I'm the cause of every experience of suffering and every experience of joy and all the rest in between that I make up about it.

I can let everything be as it is and take a look at how I'm responding to it. And choose what I make it all mean for me.

I like exercising power; I like knowing I have the choice to believe what I want to believe. I want to help create a new way of being, by transforming all that I had thought previously. It's exhilarating and freeing.

I love watching someone transform before my eyes when they give up a long-held belief that has caused them pain for years. It inspires me and others.

We simply give up one idea for another, one painful thought and embrace love instead. It's rather simple, but it really takes something to constantly be alert and responsible for our beliefs.

Choosing to be happy rather than right is not natural to human beings. Yet we can learn to accept what is, rather than raising our fists against it.

Perhaps you think acceptance would make you complacent. It's actually the most active thing you can do, to alter the context from which you live life.

You can be free of the identity that made up all that suffering if you choose to, that's how freaking powerful you are! You are playing a game of suffering, and you can choose to stop, whenever you decide you have had enough.

I personally think its way more fun to be powerful, and to know that I have the capacity to create what I want to experience and to actually make it happen.

I do it all the time.

You may not think it will work, and that's OK, but it's worth a try, wouldn't you agree?

You may not want to have to face the fear that's in your way... you may have denied that it's even there. Yet, you are smarter than that.

Intelligence, or wisdom comes from emotional and spiritual mastery over your mind.

To get there, you have to be willing to relinquish your painful identification with your bodily identity and let go of trying to solve the problem.

Then, you're good to go. (smile)

So, who am I?

CHAPTER 1

FROM BETRAYAL TO HEALING

H ave you ever been betrayed?

Has your heart ever been so wounded that it felt like it was *shattered* by someone's behavior when you were young?

Or have you ever asked yourself: "What's wrong with me?" or "Why do I seem to attract people who hurt me?"

I can relate, because I've experienced this for myself.

And even better, I've found a way out of that despair.

You see, I've helped hundreds of people in my thirty-plus years of coaching and mentoring others like you.

Before I share with you these simple methods of healing the mind, let me tell you a story.

I was raised seventh of ten children, by devout Catholic parents, in a small town just north of Bangor, Maine, called Old Town. It's a quiet place, with about 8,000 people which still looks pretty much the same as when I left back in 1977.

I remember the vibrancy of the town when we were growing up. The downtown included a drug store with a soda fountain, and a W.T.Grant department store.

The Old Town Canoe Factory and the shoe factory, where my grandmother had worked, resided on Main Street, along the Penobscot River. We were free to walk everywhere on our own any time of day or night.

I remember spending hours at the public library, sitting in small chairs for children. I loved reading, exploring the world through books, and it was a safe haven for me.

My family life was a mayhem of constant activity – kids coming and going, we had a very lively household full of love and laughter most of the time!

Dad worked for H&R Block and Mom was a secretary at the University of Maine in Orono.

Our house on Main Street, was right in the center of town next door to St. Mary's church and school. The nuns lived in a house next door to the school behind the church.

It was a six-bedroom house built by my grandfather, who died when my mother was 12. My grandmother lived there and had raised her three girls on her own.

I attended the Catholic school until the 3rd grade when it closed. I entered public school at age 10, where I was presented with an opportunity that *changed* my life.

A music teacher came and conducted a concert band and introduced all the instruments to us, and I was enamored. I begged my mother to let me play the trumpet, but she wisely suggested the clarinet, and so began what was to become my very first love…*music*.

In junior high school, my musical talent was recognized by the new band director, whose love of jazz was contagious. We started a jazz combo, performing at local events and over time, entered competitions, and my world opened up!

Music – both classical and jazz – and my faith became the focus of my life. My parents loved the standards and musicals, and I sat listening to records for hours.

On one weekend in junior high school, I attended a teen retreat called *Search* put on by the Catholic church where my friends and I spent the weekend in a nearby town. It was led by a priest from a different church and I immediately felt a connection.

I liked his sense of humor, his ability to relate to us as teens and how he talked about forgiveness and faith. Unlike my parish priest, he was funny, approachable. I remember performing with my friends, singing, and playing music in a talent show together among other activities at the retreat.

I felt this priest was someone I could confide in and I remember talking with him about fear. He called fear *"paper tigers"* and said not to worry about it too much.

A few months later, I was anxious and unable to sleep well… and not wanting to tell my parents, I decided to call this priest for counseling.

He agreed to see me, and on a spring day in early June, I walked into the rectory, a big brick building next to the much larger Catholic church further down the street from our home.

I had never been in this building before, and he greeted me at the door and welcomed me into his office.

I'll never forget his big smile, graying hair and startling blue eyes that made me feel safe and welcomed.

Before I could sit down, he shut the door and gave me a hug… then he put his hands up my back under my shirt and began kissing me on the lips!

Stunned, *I froze*.

I don't remember what happened after that…but I know it seemed to last a *long* time.

Not knowing what to do, I remember just being quiet and not saying *anything*. Shortly after, I left in a state of *confusion* and concern.

I knew one thing: I could **not** tell my parents. They were not open to criticism of the church.

Besides, what would I say? Would they even listen or believe me? I didn't think they would.

So, I *didn't tell anyone* about this horrific incident.

I put this experience out of my mind for *most* of my life, believing that it wasn't a big deal.

Mostly, I didn't think *anyone* would believe me and I was *too embarrassed* to admit it had happened to me.

Years later, when my third marriage was breaking up, this memory came to the surface in a healing session.

I had been betrayed by the priest at 14 and it had ramifications which I was only finding out about now, in my 50s.

When I turned 23, I moved to New York City to attend Brooklyn College for a master's degree in performance. There, I met my husband, a musician, producer, and keyboard player from Boston. I was head over heels in love. I moved in with him and we decided to get married after a few years together. Life was opening up and I was finally where I wanted to be. I loved studying music with the most wonderful clarinet teacher, and enjoyed all the culture and intensity of the city.

Yet, things didn't work out the way I planned.

A few years after graduation, I realized I wouldn't be able to make a living as a classical musician.

So, I gave up pursuing music as a career and worked for corporations as a technical writer for banks and insurance companies.

Within a few years, I found myself sitting all day in my cubicle staring at the clock, wondering when I could leave.

My dream to be a professional classical musician had *died*, and with it, a part of myself.

For about six months, I got more and more anxious. Many nights, I didn't sleep at all, was in a panic worrying about how I'd get through the day. But mostly scared because I didn't know what was happening to me. I would go to work exhausted and miserable, sitting in a suit and heels, spending all day writing documents that meant nothing to me.

I kept asking the question "*why am I so afraid?*"

Then I found this book "You Can Heal Your Life" by Louise Hay, which provided **the key**: that I could change my thoughts and then my life would change.

I started meditating and practicing gratitude daily...and life got better. I could sleep again.

I also changed my diet, and started seeing a holistic chiropractor. *Within weeks*, I had energy again, the fear and anxiety began to lift.

Soon afterwards, I found the book, *A Course in Miracles* and signed up for an introductory class at the New York Open Center. I began reading the lessons in *The Workbook* and found the answer to my question! In fact, all my questions were answered in this amazing book that was channeled and published just a few years earlier in New York City.

I felt loved, protected and finally, I knew that I had a purpose.

A few years later, I got pregnant and left the working world to raise my son full-time, though I still focused on meditation, using *A Course in Miracles* as my guide.

I had a mentor who helped me as I navigated the early stages of my spiritual awakening. I had been shy and introverted *most* of my life, yet gradually, I embraced my power as a healer and teacher.

Over the years since that time, I have taught *A Course in Miracles* in workshops, retreats, classes and privately. I have traveled all over the world teaching the Course and continue to do so online. It is still the most important spiritual document that has greatly altered who I am.

Years later…in 2014:

It was a sunny day in June, when after a three-day drive from Wisconsin in my red Prius, I arrived back home. It was packed with my massage table, my summer clothes, and my clarinet and saxophone. I had put everything else in storage to move back to my home state.

Maine has a magical quality; you feel it the moment you cross over the Piscataqua River Bridge. As I entered the state, a sign read "*Breathe Easy, You're in Maine*". I burst into tears.

After 40 years, I was coming home to start my life over. My kids were grown, and my third marriage had ended. I was rocked by this event that I didn't see coming. Thankfully, my brothers and sisters opened their arms to me and invited me back home.

Devastated by the loss of my father the year before, I felt like my world had *collapsed*. I wanted to be with people who loved me.

The first few months I spent with my brother and his wife at his house in Biddeford Pool. While running one morning my usual three miles on the beach, I heard a voice inside say, "*Get out of the massage business and into the transformation business.*"

I began to blog and started a website offering spiritual guidance.

The programs I now deliver came from combining my spiritual path with simple, efficient methods that heal the mind.

The *Heal Your Mind Heal Your Life* programs are designed for those who want mastery over their mind and their lives.

I have witnessed many people as they choose to step out of their fear and create what they truly desire.

It starts with creating a new relationship with your Self, thereby discovering real power. Then, you have the means to effect and alter your personal and professional life.

At the deepest level, our basic human desire is for freedom and happiness.

When you connect to your inner Self, you bypass your old patterns of behavior, to make much better decisions. Then, you can begin to alter your future.

CHAPTER 2

YOUR INNATE SPIRITUAL SELF

H ave you ever felt like you couldn't go on because of one event in your past that you haven't been able to overcome?

We each have our stories that we carry with us throughout our lives.

I haven't met anyone who could say their childhood was perfect, joyful, and uneventful. Quite the contrary, most of us have had to overcome very difficult experiences and challenges early in life.

When I was 4, my younger sister died of leukemia. Back then, there was no treatment except blood transfusions, which we know were completely ineffective. So for a few short years, my parents were overwhelmed trying to care for her, and the rest of us seven children as well.

One of my earliest memories is of my mother being sad and crying while holding me. She was listening to Tony

Bennett sing "*Smile, though your heart is breaking… you'll see the sun come shining through, for you…*"

Our past, especially early childhood, forms our personalities and how we face the world as adults. The surprising truth is that we can choose to heal no matter how we much we hurt, and how much we have fought against and tried to forget.

Your past, starting from your family of origin, your education, and your religious upbringing forms your beliefs. Add to that emotional upheaval and heartache, and often we grow up not wanting to face our past. We try to keep the past buried, especially if we endured trauma in our early years.

It's wise to bury emotional trauma when we are young – because the soul needs to survive. Yet, there comes a time when, as adults, we need to face our past, and if we choose, to heal from it.

In the last three decades, I've heard some horrifying cases of people who were badly mistreated in their childhood. It's been a journey of my own to be able to listen to stories of incest, molestation, and abuse by the people who they were supposed to trust.

My story seems trivial when I hear what these people have endured. I came from a very loving home and often feel privileged to have had a strong religious upbringing too.

Yet, no matter how painful the story, we have a choice to move beyond it, and focus on the future, using the power of mind to heal.

I'm always amazed at the *resilience* of those who do choose to heal their past and move forward.

In our spiritual awakening, we are asked to put it to the test, to see how to transcend the past and allow the miracle of grace to do its job. *A Course in Miracles* states that this is a dream of death or separation, and it takes many forms.

The only way out is through forgiveness and healing. God's will for us is perfect happiness.

Miracles are shifts in perception. They are always available when we are open to see differently. Our dream is made up of memories of pain, sorrow, loss, and hurt. Yet it can all be undone when we choose to go down a different road, and heal the past.

I have been a witness to countless miracles which have shown that we all have the ability to overcome the past and heal these memories.

We have the power of decision. We have access to the higher perspective, and we can find peace if we choose to face our fears, our resentments, and our wounds. It starts with our own self. If we don't love ourselves, it's often based on one false belief: "I'm not enough".

Perception is a choice; we can choose how we see ourselves, others, and our world. Our mind is all powerful and creative, yet healing is required.

Once we make a decision to see everything *differently*, we can then claim our infinite power.

The Self, or divine light in each of us is in a state of awareness that is very different from the identity you call yourself.

In reality, your higher Self knows exactly who it is, what it is here to do. It also knows how to accomplish what you desire, and has total love and compassion for all of life everywhere.

In essence, the higher Self is a guide for the incarnated self. It is whole and will help us rise above our past and take on the challenges of our lives. We have a chance now to face the past, the shame and the embarrassment and be healed.

When you meditate, you can communicate with that Self.

When we pay attention to our inner experiences, we have the ability to face our feelings, and connect with the Self, who knows it is whole.

For some people, this is easy, for others, they feel blocked by their beliefs or fears, or have never tried to connect with the Self. Many people find it difficult because they are afraid to make that connection.

Once you make the connection, you have access to answers and guidance for your life.

Throughout my life, I made it a priority connect to my higher Self. When I was young, I spent hours playing my clarinet, drawing, and writing. I loved being in quiet, and often escaped from the world of my family to make that connection.

I didn't know then that I was connecting with my Self, but as I grew older, I realized how my creative practices allowed me to access the light.

To connect with the Higher Self, I encourage you to try this now.

An Exercise For You to Experience The Self

Sit quietly and feel your body… experience your heart energy by placing your hand on it. Just connect to the heart. Let go of trying to do it right, it isn't about right or wrong.

Connect and feel an opening, you will simply begin to open up.

Now, feel the energy in the room and the spaces between you and the walls, the ceiling, and the floor. Give it a few minutes. Feel that expansion.

Now let that energy outside the body, connect with your heart energy.

Begin to get curious, what if I'm not confined to this body and my spiritual Self is right here?

Ask for a sign, a thought, a word, or a picture in your mind.

Don't be afraid if you feel or see something in your mind's eye.

Invite the energy of compassion. Allow it to grow. Allow your heart center to receive more energy, more love. Take it in, simply allow it to energize you.

You can ask a question from this space with a "yes or no" answer.

Just *feel* into the experience and have fun with it. Your intuition and connection to your Self is your guide to freedom. As you develop and evolve to a more aware state, your life changes.

The spiritual Self knows itself as perfect and whole. There is *nothing* missing, *nothing* lacking, it is certain of its completeness.

You can have startling results on the first try. I encourage you to go within to find the answers to your life and it's challenges. The more you connect within, the more you will gain access to your inner light and wisdom.

From the identified self's perspective, it may feel strange, or completely unnatural to you. You may be afraid of it because it is so different from the limited self. But try not to be afraid of it.

The spiritual Self knows love, light, and the infinite and eternal nature of this Reality. It does not judge you. It is compassionate and wise.

The limited self is aware of itself as a separate individual with many ideas that block the awareness of the true Self. The sum of these ideas is called your identity or "the ego".

Your limited self's identity is based on fear, confusion, doubt, and guilt.

Your identity as a separate being is always shifting and changing from one perspective to another.

Your past is made up of stories you keep telling about what happened. Yet at any given moment, you have power to free yourself from that limited perspective.

We are attached to the pain associated with these stories, yet we can detach and become free. Underneath the fear, all the anxiety and depression, resides the Self, in peace, love and wholeness.

Your spiritual Self wants the best for you as a human being and wants you to experience more joy than you could imagine.

It wants you to know through experience, how to live with freedom from fear, doubt, insecurity and lack.

You can make a decision to transform your life and all the help you need will come to your aid.

You have the power to become free to live with love, light, clarity, and joy.

It takes *commitment*, consistent *application* of the ideas presented here, and *honesty*.

If you can open up and choose to relinquish your belief in separation and lack, even by a little, you will experience success.

One decision can affect your entire life from that moment on.

Power is in the decision: I choose to be free; I have decided to put behind me the past that is already over. I choose to create a new life for myself, free of the past.

State this aloud over and over.

When we use our power, our word, and state *out loud* what we are choosing to believe, the inner voices quiet down. These attack voices are simply denying the truth and need not have power over you any longer.

Although you have been focused on beliefs and stories of victimization, albeit for many years, you can still find peace and release.

Here's a story of one of my clients.

A Student's Story

Sarah was a student in college and was having some difficulty getting to class.

She said she didn't think anyone liked her and felt all alone and rejected by everyone around her. She was in a foreign country and hadn't made a lot of friends, and whenever she went to class, she felt people around her were judging her.

I could relate to that time in my life, which was also fraught with self-doubt and loneliness.

She had a *deep belief* that she *wasn't good enough* because she been bullied in elementary school. She had been made fun of by many students when she was young.

Within the session, we released her belief: *"I'm not good enough."*

By going back to the moment and releasing that pain, she could embrace her child self again and *heal that memory*.

We talked about her being "good enough" and I encouraged her to try it on like a pair of new shoes and see what changed.

The next week, she was so excited and lit up. I asked what had happened, and she said she took my advice and all week, she walked around in her "good enough" shoes.

I was amazed at her quick progress and how completely joyful and alive she looked!

We often don't know how powerful we are, until we share the experience and the difference it made.

She learned the processes I taught her, practiced them diligently and a year or so later, graduated *with high honors!*

The "not good enough" story, which I believe most of us have, does repeat in our subconscious until we *disrupt* it. The ego always feels not "something" enough, because it does not know who it is.

One experience like Sarah's can make all the difference if you have been struggling for perhaps years with just one thought, one belief. Isn't it time to disrupt it?

A Course in Miracles states in the very beginning of Chapter One: *There is no order of difficulty in miracles... They are all the same. Miracles are natural. When they do not occur something has gone wrong.*

Message: I am meant to live from the magnificence of my authentic Self and experience miracles all the time.

Questions to think about...

Do you often feel lost, confused, or disconnected from your Self?

Do you have a spiritual practice that challenges that state of mind?

Do you want to go deeper and experience real freedom?

Are you willing to establish a daily practice?

CHAPTER 3

VICTIMHOOD

When we have been wronged, it's tempting to remain a victim.

We *all* want to be right. And we want others to suffer for what they did to us when we feel unfairly treated.

I get it, I have struggled with many relationships, divorces, a painful child custody dispute, and a molestation that could keep me bound to the past – if I let it.

Yet, in reality, being a victim is weak. There's no power in hate, or resentment, and we don't often realize it, but when we stay there, we are in a prison of our own mind.

We maintain the story to get people to agree and feel badly for us and therefore, we keep the story alive.

The result: Stay disempowered, complain, and blame the past for our experiences now.

We stay *stuck* in a past that is *already gone*, and we like it.

Why?

So that we don't have to take full responsibility for our lives.

The stories we repeatedly tell, indicate a lot about how we think about *ourselves.*

Complaining, making other people wrong, blaming – *all* come from victim.

We can even have very powerful and successful businesses and careers. Yet deep down we struggle over a painful past because we aren't aware that we are caught.

On top of that, we live in a society that rewards money, status, and fame. Sometimes, even when we achieve that, we still feel like an imposter, and can't simply accept our good fortune.

Then we judge ourselves…or make ourselves **wrong** even when things go right.

We may believe that when we achieve success, that we *don't* really deserve it.

We never seem to get a break from the incessant victim stance.

We often hide and pretend we're fine – when in truth, we're struggling just to be okay with ourselves as we are. The result is that *we suffer.*

We fail, and become frustrated by our own inability to make life work the way we think it should.

What we need is to find our ability to view our past with compassion, allow ourselves to feel the pain, and let go of playing victim. Self-acceptance, appreciation, *and* the ability to laugh at our human condition are crucial to healing.

We can take responsibility for our part, forgive ourselves and let go of self-blame.

> "Self-acceptance, appreciation, *and* the ability to laugh at our human condition are crucial to healing."
>
> ~Monica Dubay

Here's My Victim Story:

After my first divorce, I moved 1,000 miles away from New Jersey to Wisconsin.

I chose to join a spiritual community dedicated to teaching *A Course in Miracles* and spiritual awakening.

My kids were only 5 and 8 years old and the thought of taking the boys away from their father deeply troubled me. I spent months deliberating, wondering how it might work and how it would affect everyone.

But deep in my heart, I knew it was what I wanted.

My husband fought me on this point during the divorce and tried to keep me in the state of New Jersey. I was determined to step into my power to change my life.

We went into mediation and I stated the situation from my point of view. I had been lonely and unhappy and moving was what I desired.

During our first meeting, she met with us both apart, then brought us together again. She simply declared that since I was going to move to Wisconsin, we had to figure out how to handle joint custody.

We agreed, at the time of the divorce, that I could leave the state with the boys, as long as I agreed to let them come back and live with their father after 2 ½ years. This was supposed to be for a trial period of six months. Then, if they chose to come back to Wisconsin, they would be allowed to.

I never thought this would happen, since my husband had worked long hours, as a producer in his music studio for our entire relationship. I had made up a story that he didn't care about me, and he didn't really want to be there for his kids.

Yet, when the time came after two years, he had remarried, they were about to have a baby, and he set up his life so that he could work from home.

So, the boys returned for a six month trial period to live with him in New Jersey. We had a verbal agreement that if they really wanted to return to Wisconsin to be with me, they would.

After the period was over, they chose to come back to live with me, but my ex-husband *refused* to let them.

I chose to file for residential custody, thus entered into the most intense 18 months of my life.

The kids were interviewed 10 times by professionals, and we both presented evidence for the well-being of the children. My ex-husband accused me of being in a cult.

The trial lasted three days. The professionals in the case stated they believed the boys *were better off with me* because they were bonded to me. They believed it wasn't a good idea to take them from me at their young ages. The idea of the cult was brought out and there was no way to refute it. It was an interesting tactic to make me look bad. The psychologist stated that I was an ideal, loving mother and recommended that they stay with me.

I had been a very loving, full-time mother, and they had a normal life, they were in public school, and were doing very well. I left and drove back to Wisconsin, thinking I had won.

I waited for several months before the ruling of the judge.

When I got the verdict in the mail, the judge ruled that the boys should stay with their father.

I was devastated. I could see them only on their vacations and holidays. Which included only one month in the summer.

My sons went through depression, calling me for help and to come get them…and I was beside myself with deep grief.

I felt completely betrayed by my ex-husband, *and* by our judicial system, and to be honest, by God. I didn't understand how this could happen.

For many years, the anguish was *overwhelming*. Although I had tried *everything* to have the boys come back to live with me, I had failed.

I fully blamed myself.

After this *long* battle, losing custody of my boys was a betrayal. My ex-husband's breaking of his original verbal agreement **and** the judge's ruling – made *no sense* to me.

It was *especially* hard when each time they were about to leave after visiting me, my younger son would cry that he didn't want to leave! I had often had to put him on the plane while he was crying.

I don't know how I got through those moments, because my heart was breaking along with his and I couldn't relieve his pain.

The situation was unbearable especially for me because I was committed to them, yet couldn't do anything to change this situation.

I released a lot of the pain by getting a sponsor and working the 12 Steps, which helped me take responsibility for my part. Yet, I carried the guilt within me for *more than 12 years*.

Subconsciously, I thought that *"I hurt my sons"* and felt it *every time* I saw them, on *every* visit during all those years.

Yes, I had accepted that I'd chosen to leave their father and move away. Yet I blamed myself for the pain my sons went through, which seemed unending…and *I couldn't forgive myself*.

Years later, I *finally* challenged this belief.

I was tired of the story.

I used every method in *this* book to *completely* relinquish my guilt, and to step into a possibility of being free of the past.

For the boys, I believe it took about a year to adjust to the situation. They were very resilient and assured me they were okay once they got used to it. I asked them how, and they said they got a lot of support from their friends.

Now when I see them, I feel love and connection, instead of pain and sorrow.

It's been a journey of forgiveness of myself.

I *had* to let go of trying to understand what happened.

I finally claimed *my power* to stop the story, to stop blaming myself or others, *and* to move beyond it.

> "I finally claimed *my power* to stop the story, to stop blaming myself or others, *and* to move beyond it."
>
> ~Monica Dubay

If you've had an event in your life that you *haven't* been able to release, I invite you to stop, take a look and see if you can shed some light on it.

Sometimes it feels *unforgiveable*, and *impossible* to let go of. I get it.

Even if you know you have the power to change your thoughts and you've tried lot of different things, but you still feel anger whenever you think of someone that hurt you…there's more work to do.

I encourage you to *give up blame*, and stop comparing yourself to others who seem to have it easier, and know you *can* be free *when you're ready to face the pain, and ask for help.*

Victimhood takes many forms.

There is not one person on this planet who has *not* had some hardship in their lives.

The question is, what do you want?

Do you want to stay in pain…*or* use your story to heal, to recover, to inspire and help other people, to rise above the darkness and step into the light?

Victimhood implies that *others* have controlled and determined whom you experience ***yourself*** to be.

If you decide you don't like being a victim, and you realize there is an alternative, then you will seek for ways to give it up.

It would be an unfortunate *waste* to stay there and live in *that story* from which *no one* can save you. It's yours to relinquish.

Victim consciousness is a common way of life for so many, yet it *isn't* necessary to stay there.

I encourage you to have the strength and faith to step out of it *now*. Take it on as a challenge to you and see how you could write a *new story* and *create a new future* for yourself and those you love.

When you accept full responsibility for your choices, love comes to your side and shows you a whole new way of looking at yourself.

> "When you accept full responsibility for your choices, love comes to your side and shows you a whole new way of looking at yourself."
>
> ~Monica Dubay

If you knew your victim stance was the *root cause* of all your discomfort and pain, why wouldn't you simply let it go?

You will when you're done with it.

You see, we are attached to *being right* and actually *love* telling our stories.

We are human after all, and want to justify our pain, justify why we do what we do, why we believe we need to suffer.

Why?

Let's talk about this in the next section…

Undoing The Victim

Whenever you feel unfairly treated, or better or less than someone else, take a look. Are you jealous, resentful, lacking, sad, or guilty?

Being a victim has *one* belief that is hiding behind it's perspective: *I am powerless,.*

In other words…it might go something like this:

Everyone else has it easier, they didn't suffer like I did. This is just happening to me, I'm not like everyone else.

And you don't want to tell anyone because of the fact that this is happening to you, which makes you *more* vulnerable and afraid. You may be afraid of being in that situation, so <u>you don't tell anyone</u>.

This cycle keeps the problem intact and it appears that there is no escape.

Indeed, without help, we simply *stay stuck*.

Is your life painful enough to begin the spiritual work it takes to get out of that pain?

The wonderful thing is that: **Pain can be useful – *if* you use it to help yourself and others to heal.**

This takes courage and determination to put the past behind you and start anew.

Can You Stop Judging Yourself For What Happened?

When you decide to embrace full responsibility for your thoughts, and their results, and begin to do the work of changing them, your life will change.

The **painful beliefs** come from the moment <u>in the past</u> when some powerful event happened, and we came to a *belief about ourselves* and accepted it as true.

These thoughts often reside buried in the subconscious. We *bury* them for good reason, because at the time, we really didn't know what to do with the situation that happened.

How could we? We were powerless at that point in time.

We thought that *we* caused the situation and *still* blame ourselves for it.

Even as adults, we think we caused the abusive person to come into our lives and we haven't forgiven ourselves for it. We are sometimes hardest on ourselves. Even when we were victims of abuse, we still hold ourselves to blame.

We may even hold ourselves responsible for *all* that happened, though logically, it doesn't make any sense. There are two people involved in abusive situations. You both played a part.

Once you *begin* to do the inner work however, you can begin to *see* the patterns. You may see that your fear, doubt, guilt, and victimhood created a lack of power. And you don't question it.

Furthermore, you don't tell anyone because you feel so badly that this happened, **and** then your self-judgment *keeps you there.*

Besides this, you may be even more afraid of being on your own, and believe that no one else would ever love you.

You *could* run away, but where would you go? You feel utterly trapped.

From the ***victim's point of view***, there is *no hope of escape* and so you opt to stay and "fix it" or "make it work", love more, accept blame, continue to stay powerless **and** in a great deal of pain.

And somehow pretend that you're OK. When in fact, you are far from it.

Victims don't see *yet* that if they told someone else who loves them – a friend, a mentor or a health professional, they could get the help they needed.

How To Release Your Victim

Do you continually make yourself wrong?

Do you feel you are *wrong* even though you've done everything in your power to do things right?

Do you feel separated from others, like you don't fit anywhere, and are disconnected from everyone?

Or do you make up more stories of how you *don't* belong?

You feel disconnected from your real Self, because for years, you may have experienced the results: **fear** and **pain**.

The GOOD NEWS: You have the power to make up these beliefs, and you have the power to release them!

We use systematic processes to undo these beliefs that work efficiently. (These methods are in Chapter 7).

You are not powerless; you have all power to transform from fear and self-doubt. You can learn how to shift out of that pattern and accept a new one instead.

You can shift an emotional pattern and liberate yourself from a longstanding belief that caused you much pain even for many years. When you have been told these things, you may not even realize there is any other way to think about yourself, yet there is help here.

Believing Untrue Thoughts Is Debilitating, Exhausting And Causes Immense Pain

Once you learn how to let thoughts go, you will experience the release and find a new sense of power and freedom. When a long-standing belief is cleared, you then embrace a new thought that makes sense.

Yet, this may feel so unfamiliar, that you are afraid of taking that step, for fear of the unknown. A sane mind is a peaceful mind, where you allow for the future to be unlike the past. It *isn't* about fixing you, yet it is about giving up the story that keeps you in pain.

Then the miracle of grace can enlighten your mind and show you a new way to think.

Message: You can elect to change your reaction and your response to everything in your life.

Questions to think about...

What ways do you feel you are a victim?

How do these thoughts make you feel?

What would it feel like to not believe these thoughts?

Imagine your life knowing you have all power, what would change for you?

CHAPTER 4

TIME AND YOU

D o you remember a time when you didn't know how to tell time?

Wasn't it hard to learn?

How we view time is how we view ourselves, as we identify with the world and our participation in it. We agree that time is sequencing; past, present, future along a linear timeline.

When you were born, you were not under a construct of time. You were just being you. Right now, you're still you.

We think that time is passing. We all agree that there is a past, a present and a future and it is sequential. Yet, can you show me the future?

Stop and look, isn't it something you're imagining?

Do you know that you make images from your thoughts?

How about the past? Can you show me the past?

Isn't it your imagery in your memories? How do you

know that it's there, that the events really were as you remember them?

Right now, can you imagine other timelines are going on? Other people with different timelines in their minds are all happening right now.

You identify as a body in time with a past and a future. How you interact with people and the world – is the experience, the journey of being in time and space.

Your experiences keep changing, your thoughts keep changing. People in your life come and go, they are born, they grow up and they fall in love, they meet other people, they may have children, and they appear to die. It's predictable.

What we are sure of is death. A body is born, lives and then dies.

We all agree.

The Journey Goes Something Like This

You are born and are conditioned to want things, to strive to survive. You learn, you mature, you grow up and try to be happy.

You look for a way to deal within the linear framework that will bring you happiness. You find ways to survive, you fall in love, you look for happiness in so many different ways, all the while knowing that it will eventually come to an end.

Then something unexpected happens, to you or someone you love.

Maybe your parents get divorced. Or you get divorced, and your idea of love is shattered. Someone you love gets sick. And we react like it isn't supposed to happen. And it's really challenging, because it's painful to watch people suffer and to be the one suffering.

Yet, life doesn't always go the way you thought it would. Hardly ever.

These upsetting moments bring us to our knees, and they bring into question what's really going on here.

You begin to question your beliefs and the reason for your existence.

What is really going on here?

Who am I?

Your current belief system collides with Reality, and you don't like it.

You want it to work out. You want your life to be happy. You want it your way, and you don't seem to have that much control. And you may be afraid to look to question what you know out of fear of the unknown.

But then, your life begins to unravel – perhaps you lose a job or your spouse leaves you, or your kids grow up and don't want to have you in their lives.

Perhaps people reject you or you reject them, you get sick, someone you love dies, you lose custody, and your finances fall apart.

One thing is sure and constant: It's always about you.

You get the things everyone tells you will make you happy. You compare yourself to others who are 30 or 40 or 50 or 60. You have a future dream of bliss, living by the beach, drinking margaritas, and playing golf or traveling the world.

But it isn't working out that way. You may begin to wonder what's wrong with you. Why don't you fit in? Why don't you feel like you belong? Why don't you feel happy?

Our collective consciousness, societal norms, and expectations are all determined. We bought into the construct. We are told what we should **be**, **do**, and **have** by a certain point and when we don't, we feel that we've failed.

Time is a mental construct, and there isn't a fixed timeline, going from one point to the next, to the next. It's actually all happening right now, at the same time, NOW.

Your human brain can't figure this out, so bear with me.

In time and space, your life is an adventure.

You get to choose *what* you want it to be about. Everything you think is giving you the result you're experiencing. Cause and effect, it's the law.

You have an opportunity to become free, to declare what you really want, to put everything into play. To live, to love, to give.

And it all leads up to a moment of complete release, that we call death.

But what if it isn't death that releases you?

What if it's something else? What if what we call death is simply a release of limitation, like taking off a tight shoe?

When we do the inner work of releasing our beliefs and moments of separation, we learn ***how to forgive the past***. Our memories disappear, and all the pain they caused goes with them.

We awaken to Reality, right here and now.

We are truly released from the entire construct each time we forgive.

What really happens is, time seems to go backwards as we revisit a moment in the past to shine light on it and forgive it. Yet, we actually are going forward as we do that.

The miracle is the shift in perception, from living in our memories of past, to embracing the NOW.

What if time isn't sequencing at all?

A Case In Point

One of my clients was a successful businesswoman who had accomplished a great deal in her life, owning several successful businesses. She was a leader in her community whom everyone respected.

She opened up to me and said she wasn't happy, however, because of her inability to *receive* love.

When she was a child, her baby brother was killed in a car accident while she was riding in the back seat. Throughout her life, *subconsciously*, she believed she had killed her brother.

She felt she didn't deserve love, and so no matter how well she did, she always thought she would die unloved.

After releasing the belief that she killed her brother, she began to feel a lot more hopeful. She began to *expect* to be loved, and her life changed.

People began to come toward her to acknowledge how much she'd helped them and was a powerful force in their lives.

She began to take it in, to receive their love.

Within a few months, her life began to feel a lot more peaceful. She noticed this especially within her immediate family. She *felt* different, and her business picked up too.

Sometimes *one belief* can keep us from being loved.

As children, we often take on a situation unknowingly and believe we are responsible for it.

Once we forgive, or let it be "undone", we see that we were caught in an illusion. It was never true, but because we believed it, it certainly felt true to us.

It's often astounding to finally release something that you have held within and carried like a burden *all* your life. It's such a blessing to let it finally go.

The Miracle

We *don't* have a lot of control over what happens here.

We *do* have control over our own responses to the happenings of our lives. Here is where the *power of choice* truly resides.

You could be utterly devastated in one moment and then, when you choose to believe something else, you are instantly free from that devastation!

That's how the miracle works.

You might have an epiphany of release that just dawns upon you, and you see beyond the loss or disappointment.

It's almost like nothing happened! That you had made it up! It's gone.

You feel better, you can breathe again. You feel alive, free to just be yourself when a moment before, you were depressed or devastated!

What have you discovered?

You have a whole new vantage point of love and acceptance.

You may even want to run through the streets screaming, "I'm me! I'm loved! I'm whole. I know who I am, I know why I'm here! My dark dream never happened!"

Or you may just feel a calm, peaceful release, that takes you out of fear and you feel very different.

Don't be afraid, you're waking up to Reality.

It's been a long nightmare of separation, dear friends. You were always seeking the answer. And it was there, but you couldn't see it. It's OK.

It was right there all along, inside you, underneath all the fear, self-doubt, denial and guilt. Right there is a remarkable, loving, whole Self that is innocent and pure and wants to give itself to others.

The Real You

Your Self lies *underneath* all the memories that you buried.

When you can accept who you are with a new possibility of creating from this moment on, life begins again. You are, indeed, reborn in love.

That moment of liberation, and connection with all of life and humanity is powerful. You need to share it. Expression of the miracle extends it into the world where it's needed.

You may find yourself sitting on a couch for a while, and your mind just expands into peace and grace. There's no need to control anything. just allow what's happening to happen. You feel different, just calm and peaceful.

What's happening is you're becoming free of the entire construct of time and space. It may feel familiar *and* new at the same time.

The sacredness of this moment in your consciousness cannot be described in words. Your realignment with your Self is profoundly exquisite and uniquely your own experience.

Nobody understands, it's impossible to describe. You can't

really teach it or describe it. It's beyond the words that come out of your mouth. You may not have anything to say about it and yet, nothing is the same after that.

That's OK, it's natural to feel really different and strange.

My Awakening

There was a time when I realized that I had everything I wanted. I had money, kids, house, husband… everything the world tells you to want.

I had been reading *A Course in Miracles* daily for about 10 years.

Suddenly I felt a huge pain in my stomach.

I heard chanting in my head, and knew that it was from this ashram in the Catskills, from a Master I didn't really know, but had contact with her teachings and chanting.

I called a friend who lived up there and was a devotee of this Master. I told her I wanted to come and bring the kids with me. She said yes, so we went for about 10 days.

My friend welcomed me and showed me around. I had never been there before and I had rejected Eastern teachings, I just wanted *A Course in Miracles*, so I wasn't sure why I was led here.

When I entered the big hall, where the Master sat, the power of that energy was palpable. I walked in and took my seat, and the music started, and 1000 people sang "*Om Namah Shivaya*" for about 3 hours.

I just wept and wept.

I didn't know what was happening, the chanting was so beautiful and strange.

Every morning, I attended the session, and then took care of the kids in the afternoon.

I remember feeling angry that I couldn't just meditate all day like other people. When my time was almost over, someone offered to watch my boys so I could go into the meditation cave for a few minutes. I looked at the Masters pictures on the wall and asked, "Who *are* you?"

The answer came back immediately, "Who are YOU?"

I laughed! I guess I really needed to find out, because I didn't know what all this was about.

Then, I got it!

I am not my pain, it's not who I am. It's about just being myself and accepting myself exactly as I am.

I loved the ashram and energy of the place…and the devotees were so beautiful and helpful.

After 10 days, I felt very different.

I returned home, began to look at my life and reflect on the pain I had been in and then suddenly it dawned on me… it was *gone*!

I remember feeling so happy just sweeping the kitchen floor!

Something had happened… I didn't care what, because I was so happy.

A few months later, I was in my room and a powerful energy showed up. I knew I had to lie down, and I heard the voice tell me not to worry. I would be ok.

What happened over the next four days is almost unspeakable, impossible to describe. What I remember is that I started out in a void, a place where there's nothing, pure emptiness…that was the first stage – where I got very quiet inside.

I asked for more because I didn't want to stay there.

Then the energy came pouring into me in waves. I was in a completely different state.

I kept opening up more and more to receive it. I was in communication with other beings…light beings and I surrendered.

After four days of this profound experience, I felt entirely different. My body felt weird, my toes looked silly to me. I had to learn how to walk again as my body felt strange and awkward.

From that moment on, I knew life was eternal.

Love is our reality, and this dream of separation is simply that…a dream.

Everything I had read in *A Course in Miracles* was absolutely true.

We are awakened already yet dreaming of exile.

Time isn't sequential. You can awaken right now.

So, no matter where you are on your journey, you have the opportunity to live in this state of Reality. You don't have to be afraid of it, and your personal support team and guides who are with you – will lead you through it and you will emerge as your Real Self.

So what's next? You will find out. It's an adventure, remember?

Shortly after this experience, an unexpected event happened.

Jonathan Larson, a friend of ours died suddenly of a brain aneurysm. His musical, Rent, was just opening off Broadway, and my husband (at that time), had worked with him for years, arranging all his music.

At the theatre where the funeral service took place, I felt everyone's shock and sadness.

Then all this energy went right up through my crown chakra. I felt him there, and he was free! He had accomplished what he came to do.

Later, I made a connection with his spirit, and I asked him why he chose to die. He told me that he didn't need to be famous. And his legacy lives on.

Everyone who knew him was immensely sad that he had died so suddenly and yet so grateful for having known him and watched him create and give this gift of love to the world. He had lived a humble life, waiting tables at a diner and writing musicals.

Jonathan's light was this gift he brought to the planet through this powerful musical.

It went on to win a Pulitzer Prize, a Tony Award and the cast album was nominated for a Grammy Award. People would line up for hours to get tickets every day to see it over and over again, throughout its Broadway run.

I tell this story so that you'll realize that once your light is awakened, it naturally heals. Your presence and willingness are all you need.

The next chapter is all about discovering your purpose.

Questions to think about...

What tragedy or unexpected life situation caused you to question your belief in time?

Have you ever had communication with Spirit? How did it affect you?

Can you imagine living in the moment without your past?

What would it be like to step out of time?

CHAPTER 5

FINDING YOUR UNIQUE PURPOSE

What is the meaning of life? What is purpose?

It's whatever you say it is.

What if you had *that* much power, that you could determine your own purpose?

Your purpose may be to step beyond what you know about life, to risk it all for a future that is not created yet.

If you can imagine it, it's possible and can happen. Remember, your mind is all powerful, is creative *and* communicates. It's unlimited.

How do you access that power? It requires only your willingness to show up and be who you really are, a vessel of love.

Communication is sharing yourself with others. Your higher Self is always communicating. Love never stops giving, connecting, and communicating.

That's you. Your body is the form, but it can't contain you. Communication is in thoughts, ideas, and they are continuously going on. Thoughts of life, love, joining are your thoughts in Reality.

All else is just the voice of fear, but it can get in our way if we let it.

We each have innate talents and abilities.

Trying to "fit" into the world as it is currently seems to be futile. Your light doesn't "fit" anywhere, it isn't in a location.

Within the construct of time and space, you seem to appear as a body. Yet you are not limited to the body, you have an infinite ability to create, and to discover what really matters to you.

Notice how you feel about your life and what you are spending your time on.

Have you found a connection to love and are free to express that love, allowing it to move through the actions you call your life?

We struggle with purpose when we don't know who we are. When we feel separated, disconnected, and uncertain, we can't access our purpose.

We are entering a new paradigm of infinite possibility with

a challenge to create simply by deciding what we now want to engage in.

Even within the dream, there is reason to be in action and take responsibility for the dream. It's *your* world, after all.

Do you want to be an active participant who is of service to solve one of the myriad of problems we face right now?

The new paradigm is very different from the past centuries that led up to this one, where you had to slog through lots of karma to become free. You can bypass the past, by choosing to create something new in spite of your past. It's all up to you.

We have now entered a new realm outside the "box" of our old self-concepts such as: "I'm not enough", – who am I to be that powerful?"

What if you shift your consciousness in an instant?

Your denial of your own power is a constructed self-identity. Once relinquished, your world will shift along with you.

The world is a reflection of your thoughts about yourself, and is made up of your interactions, relationships, and beliefs. It's a hologram.

Remember, cause and effect are not apart.

You are connected on every level to every living thing. You are in relationship, not separate, in a state of communication with life itself. You can deny that fact, but it won't matter.

Think of gravity, it's a law. We don't have to do anything to make it work, it just works.

The old paradigm is a state of conflict, war, aggression, manipulation, selfishness, and greed that has brought us to the brink of self-annihilation. It's completely non-creative.

Your consciousness, freed from the past, opens up to a brand-new experience, where you begin to acknowledge the power of your mind to create a new world.

Can you include everyone as an important, essential part of your whole mind, along with you?

Your ultimate role may not be invented or discovered yet. Do you want to create it for yourself? We can affect people and transform our world. Indeed, we must – if we are to create a new paradigm.

I want to help you create possibilities within your mind to discover your uniqueness and bring that to the world.

You may have to make a big decision to do that, to step out of the "old you" and the old paradigm, to move forward.

Service

It's only natural to want to help share your insight and experience with the world. To be honest, I wrote this book because I *couldn't* keep all this inside me anymore. It kept me up at night, I worked on it here and there. But one day, I realized, I wanted to actually publish it. couldn't say no to that inner voice. I asked a friend for a recommendation for a publisher and the next thing I knew I hired her.

It takes something to take action and stop talking about doing something.

Do your feel other people's pain and want to do something about it?

What's your message?

Who do you want to help?

What have you learned in your life that you want to help others learn too?

Your purpose often becomes your way out of your own pain. Unencumbered by your conditioning, you become free to be yourself, living life fully.

Your feelings do matter, and they are important. Yet, the knowledge of who you are is beyond feeling. It simply is.

Don't be afraid of feeling into this new powerful way of being.

We are emotional beings and our emotions show us contrast. For example, when you're afraid you pay more attention. You begin to seek the cause of it to take care of that part of you that's afraid. Give yourself time to heal the fear and know it's OK to be afraid, especially when you're doing something you've never done before.

And then when you're relaxed and at peace, you are more focused and *clearer*.

From *clarity*, you have a lot more *power*.

When you're blocked with uncertainty, nothing really happens. You get stopped by your fear.

Case study

One of my first clients I'll call Jennifer – was struggling with chronic fatigue and didn't know what she wanted to do with her life.

She had fears of not being important, and not worthy of accomplishing her dreams.

Her mother was especially challenging, being diagnosed bipolar. When Jennifer was a young girl, she had experienced abuse. After her parents divorced, she had to grow up fast and learn to take care of herself in a very troubling environment.

When I met Jennifer, she had two children and her husband supported the family. She was about to be certified as a coach, but she wasn't sure she wanted to do that, and she was studying *A Course in Miracles*.

When we worked together, we uncovered much of what she had lived through in her past and released these memories. She also worked hard herself and learned to relinquish a lot on her own.

Over several months, she learned to master her mind, and move forward. She had a powerful awakening to who she really is.

She became strong and determined to live her own dream.

Also during this time, her husband was let go from his corporate job, and they moved and began to simplify their lives.

They explored what they wanted to do, and together, they created a new company. She became the CEO.

She and her husband now have a very successful business in the health and wellness industry.

I'll never forget her courage and her appreciation for getting the support she needed. She worked through the deepest pain and came out shining.

My Big Decision

When I was a full-time mother, I struggled for years with the feeling that I should be doing something else. I knew that I had a bigger purpose. Although I was meditating and teaching *The Course* in a small weekly group, there were many months when I thought, "This can't be my life. Where is everyone?"

I had visions of being with other people who were teaching and traveling the world, giving ourselves to this bigger dream.

Then I was told about a group at the Endeavor Academy in Wisconsin who were dedicated to living *A Course in Miracles*.

I watched a video of the Master Teacher, I immediately recognized him, and felt he knew me...but didn't know why. I had to lie down, and my energy expanded like it had during my light episode months before.

I knew my life was about to change and I was terrified because I had a young family. I couldn't imagine how I could go there. I was in a lot of conflict for several months.

I would have to put myself first – which felt very selfish to me, and went against all my upbringing. My biggest fear was that I was going to hurt my kids by making this change, and I took it very seriously.

I chose to attend the center for 30 days, which was the minimum stay required. It took a lot to arrange childcare and ask for support from my husband to do this, and it wasn't easy. My mother came for a few weeks and we had a babysitter who also stepped in.

Once I arrived, I knew I had found my place, where I belonged.

I spent those 30 days struggling with the feelings of how to change my life, how to follow my heart and make sure my kids and family were okay. I felt elated, like I finally belonged somewhere. It was so much bigger than me. Yet, I was also really scared.

As the end of the 30 days approached, I had a big decision to make.

I took a long walk along the lake knowing this was an important moment. I new that my life was about to change if I took this step.

I couldn't imagine going back to my old life of isolation when this entire community of dedicated teachers was right here.

I was afraid my husband would not let me go or let me have the kids so I could be free.

An inner voice said to me, "If you make this one choice,

you will be happy forever."

So I made that choice.

I was surprised that my husband was actually fine with the divorce. It turned out that he wanted it too. We had to work out the arrangement for the kids with a mediator... and we did that.

I moved with the kids a few months later.

My life *did* indeed change and I found what I wanted. I stayed twelve years.

The story of how this played out and what I went through after, is included in a later chapter, but I want you to know this:

> No one can advise you about what you need, to be happy and fulfilled. It's deeply personal and you will have to discover it for yourself by listening to your feelings. You have answers within you. Ask and trust your guidance.

There are no wrong choices, you will learn from every experience.

I had to discern between the voices, and ask for support, so that I was listening to the right one. I prayed that this choice would serve everyone, especially the kids.

And I had to get very honest with myself: What did I really want?

I realized it was my own transformation that I really wanted, so that I could assist others in theirs!

Love is power. It takes a great deal of courage to live with power and not be afraid of who you will become as you move forward out of the past.

When we claim our power to love ourselves and listen to our inner heart and mind, we become the way-showers.

Don't look for support from those who live in fear and defend it. They won't help.

> "No one can advise you about what you need, to be happy and fulfilled. It's deeply personal and you will have to discover it for yourself by listening to your feelings. You have answers within you. Ask and trust your guidance."
>
> ~Monica Dubay

Take a look at what your life could be if you listened to your inner voice. And remember, you matter, your life matters, and your feelings are important.

Stepping beyond your fear can feel like such a massive reach.

We have been used to living in the prison of our own self-constructed identity and have gotten used to the darkness of fear. We think we have to conform to the principles of the human condition.

A Course in Miracles teaches that we are not to conform to this world, that it is not our home. I know that feels weird to a lot of us, but how could a place of fear be home to children of God?

I invite you to take a look at *The Teachers Manual*, which gives instruction on what it means to be a teacher of God. If you feel inclined to open up to spirit, to connect and change your mind about everything, you are well on your way.

A teacher is anyone willing to be one. There are no credentials.

To become a Teacher of God is a decision to see yourself *and* someone else's needs as the same.

When you dedicate yourself to your own awakening, you naturally become a teacher.

The Course says that to teach is to demonstrate. We are all teaching all the time. What are you teaching? What are you telling everyone? What do you share with others?

When you embark on this journey, your life will be very different and may feel strange to you in the beginning.

You will have much greater mastery over your emotions.

You will know yourself as powerful and creative with your life, which brings much more certainty, focus and alignment with your Self.

What are you up against when you claim your right to be free?

That's what the next chapter is all about.

Message: The secret to happiness comes from declaring freedom from your past, from what you made up that keeps you stuck.

Questions to think about...

When were you happiest in life and what were you doing at the time?

What did that feel like?

What if you could feel that sense of purpose on a daily basis?

What would it take to make a choice for your own freedom?

CHAPTER 6

RELEASING THE SELF IDENTITY

What is the self-identity?

It is the sum total of all your beliefs and experiences and conditioning. It's also referred to as the ego. In *The Course* it is also called the self-concept.

The self-identity was the response we made to separating from our Creator. *The Course* says we had a "a tiny mad idea", a thought of separation. And in a moment of time, we separated. Or we thought we did. (refer to *The Hero of the Dream, Chapter 27.*)

Yet, there is a way out.

"When the ego was made, God placed in the mind the call to joy. This call is so strong that the ego always dissolves at its sound. That is why you must choose to hear one of two voices within you. One you made yourself, and that one is not of God. But the other is given to you by God, Who asks you only to listen to it." (refer to *The Voice for God. Chapter 5, A Course in Miracles*)

We think God rejected us, and we blamed ourselves and made up guilt. We projected that onto others and continue to maintain that position. All our fears, doubts, guilt, and denial are made up. It's all part of the dream.

To master your mind, you must choose which voice to listen to. In this chapter, I will show you how to do that.

In my work, I have discovered there are two main aspects of attack voices: The Critic and The Protector.

The Critic

When you listen to self-criticism, you are giving into shame and guilt, and its result is that you feel terrible and weak.

The critic voice is always judging you and wants you to stay small, to stay where you are, in lack, limitation and diminished power.

The attack on yourself began in your past, in your moments of pain that you naturally encountered in life. These vulnerable moments all become evidence and reasons for the inner critic to attack you.

This part of your ego is particularly *nasty*. One thing is certain: it is *not* your friend.

The critic believes you are worthless, stupid and helpless to do anything to free yourself! Mainly because you may have let it run the show for a long time, perhaps your entire life – even though its message is not true.

You are *not* the terrible, stupid, unworthy self it thinks you are…so all its criticism is just noise.

When we are in the midst of a life challenge, a transition, a divorce, an illness, a loss of finances, for example, we become vulnerable. If we give in to the critic voice during that time, it gets even ***louder***.

The inner critic says things like:

- *Who do you think you are?*
- *You can't do that, what would your family think?*
- *You aren't good enough*
- *Don't be too big for your britches*
- *You're a fraud*
- *What a dummy*
- *You're so stupid*
- *What are you thinking?*

When you listen to this voice, you will not be able to move forward with your life, you will prove that it's right by *not* challenging these thoughts.

How I Quelled My Inner Critics

My last marriage broke up suddenly, without warning, and I chose to move across the country, back to where I grew up so I could be closer to my kids. I felt a real calling to let go, take a chance, and move quickly.

I didn't know where I would live, what I would do for a living, and my kids were in New York City. I couldn't go back to live *there*.

I wanted to find a place that felt like home. So I moved back to Maine. I basically had nothing except my brothers and sisters, my car, and my trust in God.

My critic voices were loud and clear: Why didn't you see this coming? What are you going to do now? You're all alone now…etc., etc.

Here's what I did about it…

One day, I sat down and wrote all these thoughts down and challenged every single one.

I sat down, wrote them all out, and said, "Hey, listen you guys, you can have your say and then I'm going to give you all new jobs that will help me, instead of pull me into the quicksand."

I heard them out, wrote down the beliefs. Then I gave each one of them a new message to give me:

- *I'm not all alone*
- *I know what I'm doing*
- *I am making progress and meeting new people.*
- *I have courage.*
- *I'm safe and the way out is becoming clearer.*

(This method is in Chapter 7).

I felt much better and released that energy of self-doubt by giving them all new jobs to help me feel protected and loved as I moved forward. It worked!!

The Protector

Some of the inner voices are well-meaning. They are trying to protect you from further harm and insecurity.

The Protector really wants to help you and is trying to do so by keeping you playing small and staying powerless.

Its sense of threat is real, and is based on past events, so it feels completely justified in its position.

According to the Protector, taking risks is not advised, and out of fear, it wants you to stay "safe."

However, the Protector doesn't really know what safety is because it is based in fear. Staying safe is not staying in fear. It's the opposite of that.

Love and acceptance are way more powerful than fear.

If you picture *fear* as constricting and *courage* as free and more expansive, you'll get what I mean. Constriction is *never* better than release and surrendering to a new way of being.

When you listen to fear for a long time, you will believe it and make choices based on protection.

But protection from what exactly? The fear is often about an imagined future that *doesn't* exist.

The past is actually over, and once you recognize this, you don't have to stay there. You have a new choice available.

Trauma

In moments of real threat, you may have been truly harmed, and you then formed these protector voices to help you survive. It worked and it helped you to survive. The protector plays the adult who sees you need help when there was no one else to turn to, so you made up this part of you to help you.

An example: If you were emotionally or physically abused as a child and you had no one to turn to for protection, you mentally formed a protector.

You needed help, so you created an internal Protector as a solution to the situation. It was truly helpful *then*.

Yet as an adult, you can learn to heal the event and embrace the child again. Then the Protector can be released to be more helpful to you *now*.

My Past Trauma

When the priest I trusted betrayed me, I formed a belief that I *couldn't* trust men and expected betrayal from them. I wasn't aware of any of it because it was buried in my subconscious.

Yet I believed I was always seeking a strong man whom I could trust, but in my subconscious I didn't trust they would actually come through for me.

I had several relationships with older men in college where the betrayal was *repeated*. I didn't realize that I was trying to resolve that original hurt.

Throughout my life, I have faced the idea of betrayal in all my relationships.

I would give up on myself when things weren't going well, and I often felt I couldn't speak up. I would think I had to fix the issue, or I'd pretend I was OK, when the red flags were flying.

I couldn't see what I couldn't see.

I needed to find my own protection within myself. Yet this took many years…and a lot of inner work to know that this was a story, something I had made up to keep myself safe.

In trying to protect myself, I still kept the story going! I would attract yet another man who seemingly betrayed me, either by neglecting me, or cheating on me.

I now see that the Protector wasn't really protecting me but trying to help me find security by seeking someone outside of myself who would make me safe.

Looking for safety in a relationship with a partner is folly. Yet, many of us do it and it's the cause of most co-dependency. I've worked on this issue my entire life and still do, because it's one of my life lessons.

Real safety comes from knowing who I am and accepting that I am complete unto myself. No one can make me feel safe except me and my connection to my Source.

Knowing and living with the awareness of my Source is what gives me immense peace.

If you struggle with needing protection, I invite you to do some deep forgiveness work.

I finally found compassion for the priest, which took some doing, believe me. I also took responsibility for my reaction that I hadn't given up. I couldn't forgive the act itself, because as a teenager, I don't believe I caused that, or asked for it. But I could take responsibility for my reaction to it now.

How?

Well, I went to a workshop with Byron Katie, and got some help with it. It took time for me to examine how I was responsible. I filled out the Judge Your Neighbor Worksheet and one of her facilitators who was available to support the attendees spent some time with me.

After seeing that my judgment was keeping me stuck, it became clear that I was continually molesting myself with anger and resentment. I had kept it alive in my own mind, and it was hurting me! Not anyone else! The priest was long gone. I gave it up and I was healed.

The Protector has good intentions and has tried for years to keep you safe, but never letting go. Real protection comes from self-love, as we learn to forgive and accept ourselves as we are in our truth. We are whole and perfect. All else is just made up stories that keep us in pain.

We have to challenge our fears and become aware that all judgment and resentment is dangerous to our beautiful minds. We are not meant to suffer and live in the past.

(There is more about *The Work* of Byron Katie in Chapter 7.)

Can you put the past behind you?

Asking yourself this question, is the *first step* in learning to break free.

True release comes when we see that all that we experienced was for our evolutionary growth.

If it was a horrific memory, it spurred you on to go quickly through a dark experience. It may have brought you to the most important growth you could have ever asked for. To quickly learn a powerful lesson and then find a way to learn how to be courageous now.

Perhaps you're here to help others who have been through something similar once you've been healed.

What is Protection?

True protection is love. It's knowing that we always have a choice as to what we will believe. It comes from forgiveness and working out the past with courage and true understanding.

Love is power and it moves us to find solutions to the pain, and then to help others *if we choose*. I believe that we often have to move through harsh difficulties in order to awaken to resilience and find inner strength.

The door to perfect peace is either closed or opened by our own hands.

Real protection comes from breaking free of past patterns, beliefs, and tendencies to habitually blame others for our own pain.

Rewriting Your Story

You can offer a new job to your Protector, to help you open up to love from within and find real safety. You can change the story, so you feel real protection, that comes from love.

For example, to heal a Protector from keeping you "safe" by staying in fear, try something new. You can offer the protector a promotion.

Here's the way it works:

Acknowledge the Protector.

Say something like "You've done such a good job of protecting me. Thank you."

Offer it a promotion:

Now, I'm offering you a promotion. Here's your new job: Instead of keeping me in fear, I want you to help me align to my Higher Self and feel it's love and protection.

Get agreement from the Protector to take on this new role.

Finally, rewrite the story of how protection is love, and it's safe to feel loved.

Questions to think about...

What critic voices do you hear often in your mind?

What would it take for you to stop listening to them?

In what ways have you tried to protect yourself by staying small?

Can you talk to your protector, so you recognize the need for self-love rather than fear?

CHAPTER 7

RELEASING FEAR

W hen I was depressed and had *crippling* anxiety, I kept asking myself, "Why am I so afraid?"

The answer to my question was found in *A Course in Miracles*. The message was: "Fear is always a sign of strain, arising whenever what you want, conflicts with what you do." (Chapter 2 of *A Course in Miracles*, Fear and Conflict.)

You are afraid because you don't know who you are.

You are in fear and conflict in your mind, and you need to train your mind.

The correction of fear is *your* responsibility.

My thoughts and beliefs were based on the idea that "I was powerless over my life."

I had no idea who I was and what I wanted. I just knew life wasn't giving me what I thought I wanted, and I didn't know that giving up music would be the cause of my pain.

At that time in my life, I had gotten married but was alone every evening, and having given up music, I was confused and uncertain about what I wanted. And I was deeply disappointed.

Each day I would wake up *not* knowing what my life was for. I was working in corporations, walking the city streets in heels feeling like an imposter. I got so depressed, I couldn't sleep, and I would lie awake all night wondering what was the matter with me?

I found *A Course in Miracles*, and from that moment on, my life changed drastically. I had found the key to relinquishing fear.

You have to train your mind to awaken from the nightmare of fear – and *this* is precisely what happened. I read the Text and did the Workbook lessons every single day. It worked.

Fear is self-created, maintained and defended. Often, there is no real recognition that we are doing it to ourselves.

We make up a world of fear, but we cannot make it real.

The Universe does not produce fear. It exists in a state of harmony.

Fear is a response to experiencing separation from Source. "You can behave as you think you should but without entirely wanting to do so. This produces consistent behavior but entails great strain." (Chapter 2 of *A Course in Miracles*, Fear and Conflict.)

We then project our fear and objectify it. We place it outside ourselves so we can blame someone else, or a situation, the government, or a disease, a politician, or... you name it.

Once we recognize that we have a way out, and we can stop making fear real... we have a chance for a powerful and permanent transformation to occur.

Love is inherent in our very being, but when we cover it up with fear, we literally forget it's there. Love is awareness that fear is an illusion...and because we project it, it feels very real.

To overcome projection, requires that we choose a new way to be.

Fear is non-creative. It's not the opposite of love, because love has no opposite.

Fear is actually a denial of love.

Fear creates a separate identity and a separate state of mind.

So, how do you relinquish fear?

We now have more powerful methods than ever before to release fear, denial, and pain.

Mindfulness meditation, *The Course*, The Work of Byron Katie, and more are all ways to reason to the truth.

Love is all there is, fear is the denial. It's the absence of love. we have the natural ability to harness this power of love from within.

As discoveries are made about the nature of the quantum field and the multi-dimensional universe, we can become more conscious and more awake to the idea that life is eternal and has no end. We have so much support to awaken, now more than ever before.

We can step out of fear, as we relinquish our limited sense of self that we ourselves made up.

The Field of Infinite Love

The Field of Love around us is functioning perfectly with or without our awareness of its perfection. In *A Course in Miracles*, this "field" is called the Holy Spirit.

When we feel connected to the "field", we feel great, everything is working for us, we know who we are, and life is a joyful adventure.

Even when there are hardships, we can embrace them and learn to appreciate them and let them teach us important lessons in surrender.

When we feel disconnected from the "field", we feel afraid, hopeless, lost, separate, and in need of healing.

As we learn to embrace our power as healers, our innate power to connect to the "field" and each other, we let our perception be healed. We suddenly have revelations from out of the blue that all things are possible.

We are all connected in the field. That's why spontaneous healing, shifts of perception, and miracles happen!

We seem to learn through contrasting experiences so we can choose love over and over to bring about healing. As we release the past and relinquish the future, worry and resentment disappear.

Faith and healing occur when we embrace our true nature of possibilities and create something new. Forgiveness of the past is the way to relinquish the stories, and the stuck energy that keep you bound to it.

Over time, with practice, you can begin to experience more love, healing and grace, so that in the moments of disconnection, you remember how to deal with them.

Deep releases of intensity might only take a few minutes when you know how and practice using the mind to reason to the truth.

The Problem of Fear

Fear is debilitating because it erodes every aspect of our lives. It affects our money, health, relationships, and personal well-being.

When fear is predominant, we suffer.

Fear may appear as panic, rage, anger, slight agitation, annoyance, jealousy, worry, shame, guilt, or many emotional states that are painful. It can cause depression, or low physical energy and illness.

Poor mental and physical health are a result of fearful thinking.

Addictions, obsession, self-hate, are extreme states of fearful thinking.

Fear always attacks your peace of mind. You could be having a wonderful day and one thought of fear will disrupt your state of mind *entirely*. If you listen to it.

If you live with constant attack thoughts, whether it's worry or self-righteousness, you need help.

Fear is not normal. Worry is not normal, although most of us do it a lot.

If you think fear is normal, you won't look for a solution to its incessant attack. For example, if you worry about the future, you need help to learn how to train your mind to release the worry. Worry perpetuates fear and projects it into the future, which is only in your mind.

The Course asks, "Do you want to be right, or do you want to be happy?"

Justifying Fear

When you feel you are right, you justify your failure to let go of the grievance or judgment. But you are the one in pain and you are the one who is suffering. Being self-righteous is one way to ensure that you will not be happy.

Judgment is fear. When you judge someone else, that is still fear. Your need to compare and evaluate yourself to feel better is a sign of fear. It's a result of not knowing who you are and why you are in pain.

Memories

Memories of the mind are like records playing the same song that you've grown tired of, but you can't get it out of your head.

Obsessive thoughts of past events, whether mild disappointment or trauma, are memories. No matter the degree of trauma or seriousness of the event(s), when you truly want it to be healed, it can be.

There is no order of difficulty in miracles. Miracle Principle number one in *A Course in Miracles.*

Remember this.

Many people have overcome childhood trauma and suffering to live a full, mature life. They have grown into productive, content and often inspiring adults.

Fear about the future prevents you, and may I say it also robs you, from being happy right *now*. Worrying is how your mind projects the past into the future.

Worries are merely made-up ideas, or **"What if"** scenarios that play out in your mind.

And when these "what ifs" lead to negative potential scenarios, then you can see how you can't be truly happy.

Fear is a trick. You can become distracted with a future moment that *isn't* happening at all and most likely *never will*.

"The mind is very powerful and never loses its creative force. It never sleeps." (Chapter 2 of *A Course in Miracles*, Fear and Conflict.)

Worry is projecting the past into the future. You are using the power of your mind to *hurt* yourself and to focus on thoughts that mostly make no real sense. They are illusory, only in your imagination, and have no power over you.

There are no idle thoughts. Thoughts will produce something – whether something beneficial to you, or something harmful…this depends on you, what you think about, what you focus on, and how you use the power of *your* mind.

Methods to Release Fear

Life really is bigger than our current cultural understanding of what we see and feel here as separate beings. But, deep down, we remember that we are not alone, and we are not separate.

We have a memory that began before time, and it reminds us to seek for the answer, to go within and find it, to be open to a different experience. At that point, we can make a new choice and release all the *obstacles* we put in our own way. Releasing fear is one way to do that.

The power of the mind is infinite. Your mind can release fear as well as make it up!

Fear always causes stress on some level and you don't have to believe it. You have a choice and an ability to question its validity. You simply have to challenge the thought you are thinking that causes the negative reaction. Then ask yourself if the opposite of the fear-thought is equally valid.

With practice, you learn that your choice of what you want to believe is up to you.

These methods are powerful and quick, and they do not require that you accept a religious philosophy. It is more of a spiritual perspective and a psychological context, that our beliefs form the experience of our lives.

We have the power to change our beliefs.

We *can* eradicate fear if we decide that we have had enough pain, and choose to do something, to create a new way of being and behaving.

When enough people shift their fear consciousness, it affects the whole! And the possibility of peace on Earth becomes a reality.

The ultimate question is: Who are you *without* your fear thoughts?

Think of fear as a bunch of thoughts that you can choose to believe or not, and it will help you begin.

> "We *can* eradicate fear if we decide that we have had enough pain, and choose to do something, to create a new way of being and behaving."
>
> ~Monica Dubay

Denial

People often deny they are afraid, yet the energy I experience with them is literally one of "shaking in terror".

Anger, self- righteousness, deep resentment, shame, rage, and other intense states can often cover up the real underlying fear.

You feel threatened, so you defend yourself. You dig your heels in and "hold your ground" and stay in control.

When you release fear, however, your energy expands. You feel released, loved, held in an energy of grace, uplifted by something beyond your own ideas.

It's an entirely different experience from denial.

Using simple methods, we give ourselves permission to think a new thought, and fear can be released miraculously. We give it up when we are *willing* to let it go, by feeling it first, then noticing what the thought is, and then seeing it differently.

Your life experience is the result of what you believe about yourself and how the "world" is.

It took a long time to convince you that fear is *normal*, so it may take a while for you to realize it ***isn't***. Because fear is simply a set of ideas that you made up or bought into once you were conditioned in your childhood.

You always have the choice in every moment to see it differently, to ask for a miracle of release, and to forgive. Your mind is creative, it isn't designed to hold onto thoughts, especially those that cause pain.

It's much easier to let go than hold onto a heavy burden of fear or guilt. You just need to learn how.

Forgiveness Is the Key to Happiness

Forgiveness is how we can step out of fear *forever*. Imagine carrying a big boulder on your back, and it's familiar because it's been there a long time. Now, imagine choosing to let it drop and dissolve into the earth and disappear.

That's how easy it is to forgive, or it can be.

Be willing to look within, ask for a miracle, and let it release. We have to practice it continuously, until we feel released, and the memory is gone.

The entire Course in Miracles is teaching about forgiveness. All 365 Lessons.

Ultimately, when we truly let go of a resentment, we see that there was nothing to forgive.

Our imagined hurts and resentments are thoughts that cause our pain. Yes, they come from something that happened. But it's not happening now. And can you actually prove that it happened the way you remember it? Isn't that still your perception?

Here's how I learned how to forgive when I was completely certain that I was right and didn't want to.

My Story of Forgiveness

I had picked up the boys from the airport, knowing we would have a week's vacation together after losing residential custody of them a few months before.

My parents and I had planned to be together for a week in Florida, and I was still devastated from the battle I had been through over the previous two years.

I was still upset, betrayed and devastated and there was one person I just couldn't forgive – my ex-husband.

Months earlier, I had done some 12 Step work and taken full responsibility for the horrific experience of going to trial to fight for custody of my kids.

After a grueling 18 months of this legal battle, I *lost* residential custody. I was shocked and urgently needed help.

I found a sponsor and asked her to help me work on myself. During this work, I wrote out all my feelings, and the resentment I felt for everyone involved. I was able to see that my part in it had been thinking that I was right and justifying my position.

I wanted to protect my kids and to give them the love I had committed to since they were born. I couldn't see how I would live without their constant presence, and my being there for them every day, or how they would survive without me. It made absolutely no sense to me.

From doing the 12 Step work, I saw how I'd been afraid and self-seeking because I wanted my kids with me. In reality, I didn't know what the best outcome was supposed to be, I just knew what I thought it should be.

With the help of my sponsor, I got to the step where I asked to be relieved of my "defects of character" – selfishness, fear, control and anger.

What tremendous relief I felt when I gave up these "defects"…and knew I was going to be alright!

I would have to stay in the moment, and let this all unfold, yet I *finally* got to a place of acceptance, and felt something *shift* inside me.

Then I got to Step 8: Become willing to make amends.

Oh, I didn't believe I could do this. I stayed there for months. You see, I wasn't *willing*.

I had accepted the situation but wasn't willing to forgive

my ex-husband. I still felt the boys should be with me and the deep wound at that time was still pretty raw.

But when I saw the boys come through the gate that day in Florida, I suddenly realized I hadn't lost them, here they were, and we were going on vacation together with my family.

A voice inside said, "Tell their Dad that you forgive him." Suddenly, I could feel my heart open up and I felt a surge of energy come through me.

So I called him to say that they had arrived – and then didn't know what to say next… so I just let the words come out of my mouth.

I told him that I was glad he fought for custody, that it meant he was a great Dad, and they knew he wanted them. He thanked me and said it was nice to hear. It all happened so quickly that I had to cry *and* laugh out loud. It was hugely significant because in that *one* moment, I released the resentment.

I felt the anger release – it was simply gone after I hung up! And in that moment, a voice said to me, "It took you long enough!"

I laughed at myself – and thought about how we hold onto painful thoughts, resentments, betrayals. And the entire time they keep us *stuck* and *in pain*.

I find it astounding how simple and yet, how important it is to learn how to forgive *deep resentment*, especially when it seems impossible.

> "Forgiveness is how we can step out of fear *forever*." ~Monica Dubay

You see, I *didn't* know how to do it, and I didn't *have* to know, but I *became willing* to be shown.

If we can't forgive when the pain is too great, remember there is a power within that can do it for us when we falter.

Remember: Love heals all wounds regardless of the intensity of emotional pain.

And for this I am truly grateful.

> "If we can't forgive when the pain is too great, remember there is a power within that can do it for us when we falter." ~Monica Dubay

How to Forgive Something You Can't Forgive

If you want peace, joy, and happiness to be a real experience then you must learn to forgive what is over and gone.

Here's one very powerful method that works every time.

Easy Forgiveness Method

I learned this from a healer named Judy White Hosker.

Put that person's image in front of you either with a real photograph, or by visualizing them standing in front of you.

Quiet your inner voices, and expand into your Self, the all-knowing, loving, compassionate Self.

Feel your heart energy shift to expand out from your body.

Connect with that "field" of love.

Look at the person and state out loud three times.

1. *I forgive you for hurting me. 3x*
2. *Thank you for forgiving me. 3x*
3. *I forgive myself. 3x*

Let the release occur in the quiet space and know you *are* free.

You can do this anywhere, anytime, and in any situation and it will free you.

Remember, you have all power in Heaven and Earth.

Here's a process that works for beliefs and thoughts that keep you stuck

To forgive a belief, you can use *The Work of Byron Katie*. For complimentary *Judge Your Neighbor Worksheets*, and more information, contact Thework.com.

1. Notice what thought brings you pain whenever you think of it.
2. Write it down.
3. Now ask yourself: Is it true? Yes or no.
4. Now ask yourself: Are you absolutely sure it's true? Yes or no.
5. Now ask: How do you react when you believe it? Write down the feelings the physical response, energy, and notice the images.
6. Now ask yourself: Who would you be without this thought? How would you feel if you didn't believe it, what would be different? Imagine what would change inside you if you simply did not believe that thought. Give it time to come to you.
7. Write it down.
8. Turn it around. Now begin to explore how the

opposite of that thought could be true. Write it down.

What if that thought were true? How would it feel? What would be different? Let's say it is true, now what? Give it time and explore this fully.

You will quickly see that the opposite to *that* thought could also be true. And you may prefer to think that thought. It's up to you because your power is in choosing which thoughts you want to think.

When you don't know you have a choice, you stay stuck. But when you know you do have a choice, you embrace that power and become free.

Another quick method to release fear is by forgiving yourself

Write down the thought you are thinking. Remember, it's just a thought.

Can you forgive yourself for believing a thought?

State out loud:

I forgive myself for believing _____
(the thought). It's not true. I thank God it's not true.

I release it from my subconscious mind now.

Take a deep breath and release it with the exhale.

Repeat until you feel it's gone.

Now state the opposite and embrace it.

Remember, false ideas are never true, so they *can* be released instantly.

Questions to think about...

Can you take the time to do a 10-minute process when you feel stuck?

What would it take for you to spend 20-30 minutes per day on forgiving the past?

Are you willing to try one of these methods right now and see how you feel?

CHAPTER 8

RELEASING GUILT

The deepest problem human beings face is a subconscious guilt that we have done something wrong.

The story goes something like this…

We had a small desire to be separate, and from that one idea, we made a world where we could hide ourselves from our Creator. We experienced the shock of "separation". Then we immediately felt guilty for having done something so egregious, that we believed we would be punished.

We couldn't stand the guilt of what we thought occurred, so we projected it out onto others, and made up a God who would punish us.

We didn't want to take responsibility for the mistake, so we continued to keep it by telling the story of how we are guilty and can do nothing about it!

Why do we keep this story alive?

I believe that when we blame, we *avoid* our power.

This may surprise you, but we actually *prefer* being powerless, so that <u>we don't have to take responsibility for what we think</u>.

Sometimes people just give up and stay in depression, while maintaining a lack of responsibility. They don't like to hear that, though.

When your pain threshold is reached, you *finally* ask the questions: Am I guilty? Is it really true? I am guilty of committing this terrible, unforgiveable act?

Am I actually successful at separating from God, from Reality and life itself?

The answer, my friend, is no, of course not.

It's impossible for you to be separate from the Creator.

But you could choose to believe that you are…and have done so. Most of this is buried in the subconscious, and may not even realize you believe it.

Without guilt, you would be infinitely happy.

Guilt is often pushed down, denied, turned into shame, and used to blame others or yourself. You make up endless scenarios to assuage the guilt, but never actually let it go.

Underneath the guilt, there is a *real fear*.

You have a serious problem and if you admitted it, you would not know what to do.

The guilt becomes unbearable and at its deepest layer, turns to self-hatred. If you face it, you won't have to let it debilitate you from being powerful nor from taking charge of your life.

This subconscious guilt can be terrifying. Self-hatred is at the bottom of it and can be relinquished.

Once you get to *that*, it's so deeply ingrained in your consciousness, that you may need additional support to free yourself.

No matter what occurred in the past, within your nightmare, you are not guilty. Yes, you have made mistakes – we all have.

You are already forgiven, however, because the Creator knows you perfectly and knows that you are dreaming a dream of guilt. You are not condemned for dreaming a dream of separation.

If you do judge yourself and think you deserve punishment, you *will* have it.

But it's all *self-inflicted*.

"From what you want, God cannot save you." – Free will is a law.

The healing of this deep subconscious guilt allows you to learn that you, yourself, are completely innocent. From this vantage point, you find a new way of *seeing*, of *being* and of *loving* yourself and others.

You recognize that your only problem has already been solved for you.

(See Lesson 80, Let me recognize my problems have been solved in *A Course in Miracles* for further understanding.)

The Source of the universe is only love, and love is merciful, kind, all knowing, forgiving and free from the tyranny of guilt.

All the pain in the world, which comes from guilt can be undone by the infinite power of love.

Love knows not of guilt and only knows that you are an extension of Itself, being Love forever always.

When the false self dissolves, guilt goes along with it. Then you'll discover that underneath all that drama and pain, there is only love.

No soul is ever lost, no soul is ever condemned.

Once you realize this, you can begin to wake up to the idea that you were dreaming this dream of guilt and you can choose to stop.

Love is the answer.

It frees us to become *aware*, *awake*, and more *in touch* with Reality.

We are all "driven mad" by guilt, on some level. But I ask you to consider that even your deepest secret can be healed.

All we need is a supportive person, another human being who is capable of listening and staying present *without* judgment.

Case Study

I had a client who had an abusive mother. Then she married an abusive man who also sexually abused the children. She had split with him 17 years earlier, and she had successfully raised the kids on her own.

She was now remarried to a loving partner. She had *no* idea about the sexual abuse of the children until she had left him and started over.

She came to me having healed a lot of the pain, but still stuck with intense self-judgment. She could not forgive herself for causing *so* much pain to her children.

Her thought was "I should have seen it".

This *one thought* was causing her grief, pain, and self-hatred. Her thoughts about herself were punishing, condemning, and debilitating.

Interestingly, she had become a holistic healer herself.

As I worked with her, she began to realize that the thought: "I should have seen it", was the cause of tremendous guilt.

She was not going to be the healer she wanted to be, if she did not release the guilt from her mind. Yet, she really believed she deserved to be punished!

The deep pain surfaced, during the telling of the story, we allowed the light to shine on it. I challenged her to give up punishing herself.

When asked, had she had enough?

I pointed out that even if she couldn't forgive herself, she could ask her guides to do it, to help her see what's real.

It was then that she was able to experience the rage, and the immense pain of what had happened.

Once her thought was brought to the surface, that she shouldn't have known, because she didn't know, she could accept that was true. Then, she set herself free from self-judgment. She is now free to create a more loving life for herself and her children.

Sometimes we think that our painful memories from the past are the exception. We say things like: "Well, you just don't understand. This is different, my situation is different. This is completely unforgiveable."

But nothing is unforgiveable. Even the darkest, most egregious sin (mistake), that we judge ourselves for, can be undone.

Guilt can stay with us for lifetimes, maintaining suffering. But, in truth, it is still part of the denial of who we are.

We are not meant to suffer with ideas that are not true.

It's a choice to continue to punish ourselves with guilt or not. We can walk the world free of guilt when we *choose* to give it up.

Where It Begins

The ultimate guilt told in our religions and mythology, needs close examination if we are to be free.

Although the mythology says we were cast of out of the Garden of Eden, I do not believe in a God that would cast me out of love.

I believe it's an allegory of rejection and blame. God did this to me. God hates me. God is judging me.

These are scary thoughts, and many people suffer with them as a result of conditioning. Even as a young girl in Catholic school, this made no sense to me.

I remember thinking: If God loves me, how could he reject me?

How could a loving creator cast you out then judge you for it? It makes no sense.

I believe that God does not judge, as Jesus taught us. God is love.

I believe what *The Course* states. God has already saved us from our nightmare of separation. It's over. We are just beginning to accept the Atonement for ourselves, which is our only function.

The Kingdom is a state of mind – of oneness with God, with Reality and with Love. It's what we are. Whatever your beliefs, you can forgive the past.

The message of the New Testament is God is love. Our Reality is oneness with this benevolent God. He has never condemned you.

God does not forgive, for He has never condemned.

Forgiveness stops the idea of guilt within your mind.

Once you recognize your guilt comes from a story that you were told, you can begin to forgive yourself for believing that you are guilty for something you didn't do.

Guilt breeds the tyranny of self-abasement and punishment.

There is no love in guilt. There is freedom in relinquishing it from your mind.

To forgive yourself for the "mistakes" of the past, means simply that you forgot who you were, and then you bought into a story. You can always remember that it's not true.

Letting love *replace* guilt is the answer.

The simplest way is to remember that you did not create yourself, God did.

God is love.

To "turn the other cheek" means to show that you are not hurt, not betrayed. To "go the extra mile", is to go beyond your belief, and to expand your love for yourself and others. Learn to go the extra mile, and love your neighbor, as you love yourself.

What if your life has much more meaning than you realized?

The ultimate forgiveness is that your story of guilt was never true. You can *finally* find your way out of the whole thing if you choose to.

Allow the idea that it's possible that your guilt and pain brought you to this moment right now. And it all worked. Which means that everything has helped you to become free. All the hardship, all the dark dreams, and challenging relationships helped you awaken.

So you can be grateful for every experience. Gratitude for life itself is the way out.

"Nothing can hurt you unless you give it the power to do so." *A Course in Miracles*, Chapter 20, Entering the Ark.

Forgiveness Works

Forgiveness work is powerful, deep, and permanent. It's worth every second of effort to release your mind from the guilty stories that plague you. Freedom lies within love's embrace, because once you are forgiven, you can begin to live again.

It's your choice to be free of your suffering, by letting go of guilt. Once you are released, you are forgiven, and suffering ceases to have any meaning.

And when we share our experience of forgiveness, we extend miracles!

"You who were a prisoner in separation are now made free in Paradise." *A Course in Miracles*, Chapter 20, The Vision of Holiness.

Questions to think about...

What if you could accept your innocence instead of guilt, what would change, how would you feel about yourself?

If you knew you were already forgiven for your deepest, darkest secret, what would you feel?

What's that secret? Write it down and forgive yourself for believing it. See what happens.

How would you show up in your relationships differently? How would they benefit from your release of guilt?

CHAPTER 9

RELEASING JUDGMENT

One of the most difficult challenges when we become more self-aware is to stop judging. You almost have to stop thinking entirely, to stop judging yourself *and* others.

Judgment makes up the false self – it's always condemning, or making someone wrong. It comes from the incessant need to be right and to have your opinions validated.

I understand that we often think our opinions are true, because we believe them. We may think we're seeking respect, but underneath, we are often seeking approval.

If you were judged harshly growing up, you probably have high expectations of yourself. You keep trying to perfect yourself, to make up for being mistreated.

You may have learned to compensate for this by becoming a loner, an introvert, **or** a high achiever. You always try to better yourself – because deep down, you don't feel valued or worthy.

Case Study

I've had many clients who were traumatized by severe judgment from their parents. One was a woman whom I'll call Heather.

She came to me when she had gotten laid off and was close to retirement. She did not want to retire yet and didn't know what she wanted to do next.

Heather's mother was abusive, and she had to leave home at an early age to get away. She flunked out of college, but then got herself together and ended up earning a PhD.

She had married two men who did not treat her well, and when she came to me, she said she wanted to find her life purpose.

Because of the abuse and deep anger, she did not allow herself to feel real love *for herself*. She made up rules for her life and didn't understand why life had been so difficult for her.

Though she had excelled financially and had freed herself from two abusive men, in spite of these amazing accomplishments, she wasn't able to feel good about herself.

When trauma causes deep pain, we must tread lightly and find ways to connect to the inner parts that were hurt.

The way out of deep pain and self-judgment is self-love.

I helped her see that the work she needed to do was internal.

Purpose resides underneath all the anger and resentment and we have to heal that first. I helped her to see it was important for her to give herself time to recover and be okay with herself.

It was difficult for her to trust in the process and let go. I understand that, and I get how confronting it is. Willingness is required.

We sometimes try to make our lives work without facing the cause of suffering. Yet, the deeper wounds keep us in pain, and they become the drivers of our lives.

On this journey, we can learn to release the harsh rules *we* made_up to obey. Giving up self-judgment is a *huge* change for many people, especially abuse victims.

We need compassion and self-awareness. Once we have found these, the deeper healing can take place.

If you were abused, resisting your healing work is not going to help you move forward. Bitterness, and self-judgment actually mirror the harshness we experienced in our childhood. Being overly harsh with ourselves isn't helpful and needs attention to be healed.

My Experience

I had a loving home, but there were several times when my mother criticized me. Yet, I continued to compensate for it myself, by trying to be "good" or better than others. I would try to fix relationships and heal everyone, be the peacemaker.

I had a harsh kindergarten teacher who was very strict and mean. So from the moment I left home, I didn't feel safe. I then had nuns who were also really good at instilling fear in young children. This pattern kept repeating in my life with a few music teachers and conductors.

When we learn to be compassionate toward ourselves, the pain can be released, and we soften. The heart center can open to a new way of being, where we stop judging what has occurred and receive our own mercy.

If you feel resentment for being treated unfairly, you are not free. Your obsessive thoughts of a situation do nothing but reinforce the pain, and it's a double bind.

You will be taken care of perfectly in your healing of the deepest judgments and resentment. You cannot change the outcome, but you can change your reaction to the outcome.

The hardest lessons are the ones that bring the deepest pain, and they are also the ones that set us free.

Doing deep work *changes you*…even the most traumatic events *can* be forgiven. Your beliefs are *still* the cause of your pain.

I know how hard it can be to hear this, but after the event is over, no matter how extreme the situation, love wins when we forgive. We win. We get to be free.

We can learn to evolve into compassionate, more sensitive human beings.

> "Love wins when we forgive. We win. We get to be free."
>
> ~Monica Dubay

Hitting the lowest point, when you don't have anywhere to go but inside and surrender, is a turning point in your awakening.

I know it doesn't feel that way because it is a "bottom".

But consider this idea: The bottom can be a springboard that could catapult you into a realm of pure love and self-awareness and connection with your Creator.

It can change your life entirely! But you won't know that until you experience the release.

You can't get yourself out of it. You need help. Surrender at this point is critical.

The ego finally dissolves when we stop trying to solve our own problem.

Questions to think about...

Do you judge yourself?

How does judging yourself make you feel?

Did someone from your past judge you harshly?

Can you find a way to forgive yourself for perpetuating this situation?

What life lessons have you learned from this event?

CHAPTER 10

INTUITION AND
THE REAL YOU

Light energy and innate intelligence comprise our reality.

All of the information you seek is within your personal energy field. Your energy field contains all the DNA, all the information that made your body.

Your mind is *not* contained within the body but encompasses your entire energy field. It is multi-dimensional and therefore, not limited to the three dimension that our physical eyes see.

Because your mind is all powerful, you have the creative ability to believe and therefore experience what you choose. And belief is powerful indeed. Your mind is always creating.

When you do the deep inner work to release your own conflictual beliefs, your life changes dramatically.

You'll feel a much greater sense of peace and well-being on a daily basis.

The inner work has rewards that are unlike anything you have ever experienced! You'll laugh more, and you'll feel a lot lighter as your energy field is freed up.

As you begin to experience the release of your belief patterns, you'll learn that *letting go* is easier than *doing battle.* You'll have a lot more energy to use for creating. Your resistance, anger and fear *disappear.*

Your energy field becomes more balanced, your emotions are peaceful, and you have nothing to prove. Life becomes an interesting play of ideas – and over time, your bodily concerns melt away.

Happiness become effortless, although it may have taken great suffering to bring you to this state.

Once here, joy is natural. All ideas of lack, loss, death, and suffering are gone.

To live in harmony with yourself is worth every moment of the work you do to release of fear, doubt, guilt, and judgment. Once you have reconnected with your Higher Self, you feel the joy of life.

There is immense power in knowing *who* you are and *what* you are meant to do. Yet you were blocked by your past and your beliefs prior to doing the essential internal work.

When you feel resistance, deep fear, anger, guilt, or shame, you know you have work to do. The only way out is *through* it.

How you do this is up to you.

This book includes some of the methods that I have found helpful. You can try them out, and can get help when you need it.

You need to decide what works most efficiently for you.

There are many teachers and many methods. I suggest that you find one you resonate with.

Yet don't be surprised when after a while they disappoint you, because every student comes to a teacher to learn what they know, and once they do, they must move on to grow further.

We always outgrow our teachers, and Masters won't let you idolize them. You probably will, but be aware of this tendency. Why should you idolize someone just because they are helping you. A true teacher only wants you to be *free* of all attachments to relationships including the one with them.

Intuition

Inner knowing or intuition, plays an integral part in the "undoing" of your mind. As you develop intuition, you learn to trust it and to allow it to guide you into a new way of being.

You'll find your own innate power to go within, and discover the blocks you have been harboring. This book is written to help you become much more self-aware and able to trust your inner knowing.

Use your own discernment and you will find your way. Mistakes are learning experiences, so don't judge yourself for learning through contrasting experiences.

Your Higher Self is your greatest teacher.

The Intellect

Your intellect can help you reason with the truth as your intuitive ability is developed. Both the intellect, and reasoning mind can be *helpful* to you if you allow it.

As we awaken and experience more light and more inner truth, we step out of linear thought.

Time is used for your transformation, and speeds up causing you to experience *miracles of release!* The miracle causes shifts in time, collapsing it the more you change your mind.

Then, time ceases to sequence in your mind. You know who you are, why you are here, and the inner world of light and love has no edges, no time, no limits!

You then come into a new light of reality as your own consciousness.

Once aligned, you can receive *all* the information at *any time* you want. Teachers, coaches, and guides show up right when you need them.

You can channel or intuit information from a new place in your mind, where creativity is flowing. You'll have a moment of revelation when a sudden answer comes to you out of nowhere. You've often had this experience before, whenever you were open enough to receive a new way of looking at a problem.

The resolving of your human condition is always about releasing your perception and acting upon the information that you receive intuitively. Your Self has all the solutions to your "seeming problems".

The universe is benevolent, the Creator loves you, and wants you to be happy, free and in complete alignment with your Self, because it knows YOU as that Self.

You are denying it with your false beliefs, but those beliefs are not true.

Problem Solving

I know many of us have defined ourselves by the ability to solve problems with our intellect. But that just creates another problem, and you will always find another one to solve.

So, here is my advice to you problem solvers out there: Stop trying to solve your problem, no matter what it is. Instead, let the real answer come to you through your intuitive connection.

If you insist that the problem is real, is very serious and is causing you pain, you will not be able to hear the answer.

But if you are willing to relax the need for a quick fix, you'll stay open.

You can develop your intuitive ability at any time. The more attention you give your intuitive power, the more developed it becomes, just as a muscle exercised gets stronger. Once you learn to live with your connection to your Self, which is innate in you, you become aware and alive.

Artists, creative people, innovators, inventors, musicians,

and entrepreneurs are good at connecting to their intuition.

It's joyful work, knowing you are inspired and in connection to the Real You who sees all, knows all and guides you through the maze of your life.

With all the choices you need to make throughout your life, your connection to the Self shows you which way to go. You can learn how to proceed, and to open new doors when one closes. I believe you naturally feel aligned, on purpose, in harmony with your Self and others.

The Higher Self and You

Your Higher Self is not the opposite of you but is You. The Higher Self vibrates at a higher frequency and is in a different state of consciousness and dimension. It is not contained within a body but resides in yours.

Here's something to discover: You don't have two selves.

You, who you really are, the Self resides within. You made a false self, but it was never you. This false you is not to be rejected but loved and included. Nothing happened, you didn't split yourself into two selves, you just think you did.

Your perception of you and your little self, was just that, a perception, a mistaken identity based on limitation. The little self is living the journey perfectly.

The bodily identification brings about limited awareness and suffering. It isn't the real You, but you have constructed it to deny the real You. You cannot change what you are in truth, that is why it is so energizing to find that <u>You have always been You</u>.

You were never not You.

You are and always have been connected to Source.

Once you recognize this, all of your faculties and inherent abilities you may have denied previously, are brought "on-line". You are a fully-functioning being with abilities far beyond your third dimensional understanding.

As you begin to discover these innate abilities, you will begin to realize just how infinite you are.

"All power is given unto you in Heaven and Earth", means you are not limited in any way by your perception. Perception comes from not understanding the whole.

Because you have believed it for so long, you still do believe it. Yet, your belief can change when you decide you want a new experience.

The power of your mind to choose and decide what you want is always with you. You can decide to become aware of the unlimited nature of Reality.

My Intuitive Connection

When I first found my intuitive connection and *A Course in Miracles* at the age of 30, I was overwhelmed with gratitude. I wanted to tell everyone that I had found the Answer. I felt entirely different from the depressed, fearful me – I was elated and overjoyed!

I could not make total sense of why I felt so free, but I didn't really care. I was free of the deep anguish that had engulfed me for many months of deep depression.

I knew my life would be very different from then on, just by feeling the possibility of it and the almost overwhelming sense of joy that I could tap into.

My mind kept shifting rapidly, as I read *A Course in Miracles* and heard the inner voice begin to speak to me. It was loud and clear.

The energy of my consciousness shifted out of doubt and fear – to love, freedom and happiness and I knew I was given another chance.

The energy of my body changed too, as I began to eat differently and do yoga more diligently. I went to chiropractors and my spine freed up as well. My health came back, and I had so much energy, I couldn't believe it!

I began to understand what my life purpose was about. I was hearing the voice, writing down what information I heard and taking it all in. I followed its direction and quit one job and took another. I volunteered for people with AIDS and began to teach the Course in a small group.

I was connected again to my inner guidance system. I took actions based upon that inner guidance, and *my life changed quickly.*

I felt like a completely new person. I felt the creative power of my mind open up to all possibilities. I began to paint, to write, and changed my job to work helping others in service.

Then, after two miscarriages that had occurred before this time, I got pregnant and was so incredibly grateful to become a mother. I entered that precious time of giving birth to my two amazing sons and gave my whole heart and soul to their upbringing.

I felt on top of the world and knew I was here to love, to have compassion, to be *fully* on the spiritual path.

I began connecting with others who were on the path and made friends with them.

Life became an interesting adventure, it was and continues to be full of surprises as I help others to find their intuitive connection to their Higher Self and their purpose.

I love my life now because I know with total certainty who I am.

You can know this too. You just have to want it and be willing to do what it takes to awaken.

Tapping into The Higher Energy

When you are in a receptive state of mind, you begin to feel the higher frequencies flow through you. When you have been operating from a very limited viewpoint, like one key on the keyboard of 88 keys, you can only hear that *one* note.

In reality, you have a much wider range of communicative ability that's beyond that limitation. You may feel the answers come to help you heal the mind and not know how you know the answer. You just do.

If you have ever been in the presence of an awakened Master, you'll know the energy they generate. It heals and awakens those who come close to them. They know who they are and are very aware of their assignment. They are in total service without any personal agenda.

They extend the creative power of the Universe from their hearts and minds. They don't choose their assignment; it chooses them, and they gratefully accept and carry it out no matter what it costs them personally.

We all have the ability to lead, but saying yes to leadership comes with responsibility.

Mastery of Life

What does it mean to master your life? What does it mean to lead?

Is it possible that your life is beyond your own ideas about it?

As you accept the truth of who you are, your Higher Self is not concerned with just you. Humanity is in need of leaders. Those who are willing to buck the status quo and take a chance on giving to those who can learn something from you. When you accept your role as leader, you naturally become a beacon for others.

Leadership is about saying yes, when doing so is for something beyond you and your personal life.

It's risky. It requires that you have something at stake. You are willing to forego personal comfort to accomplish something greater than yourself.

Your compassion and love for humanity drives your life, and your willingness to show up when others won't, because it might just help someone who suffers with a similar problem become free.

The reward is in the giving of yourself to a higher cause. There is a plan of awakening. It's up to us to embrace it and take our place in it.

God only gives. Giving is the answer to most of our problems. If everyone were to give of him or herself in a way that makes them joyful, not out of sacrifice, but with compassion and care, the world would change rapidly.

Fear can stop you if you let it, but will eventually go. Anything of real value is given from a higher place, and is often freely given you by someone else who was willing to show up for you.

The time is set by you, and you will awaken to your purpose, your role in the plan at the appointed time. So rest assured, you are on the right track, you can't fail. You are given *all* you need for your transformation into the real You and your role will appear. Sometimes it will startle you because you didn't see it coming.

You may not even know you have agreed until the moment you take a chance. We all have a gift to give. When we choose to give it, we get happy.

Judging Yourself and Comparing Yourself with Others

Worrying about whether your awakening has happened yet or not is comparison and ego. If you accept and trust that you are in the perfect time and place for your awakening to occur no matter what the circumstances, you will be fine.

Remember, your attack on yourself is all that you are giving up.

Your limited perception is always too small to understand the big picture, so you don't have to try to "figure it out". The constructed identity is what tries to figure out what reality is, and it will never know. Even the attempt is ludicrous.

The real You is not having a dilemma – it is perfectly at peace. So you don't have to listen to this fearful voice anymore and you always have choice…ask yourself: What do I want?

Keep asking yourself this when you are tempted to believe the lies that you're not _____ enough.

You may have glimpses of a higher vision for your life. Or you may have a spontaneous healing, or a wonderful feeling of joining, of falling in love. You become part of something bigger than yourself and you just let go into it.

Your perceptions melt away. Your light expands into a new understanding and you feel the incredible joy of awakening.

I've had many episodes of being taken into a higher dimensional reality as I slipped through the "veil" of separation. I was exceedingly happy, knowing that is who I am, and I was told that this state of love and joy never ends.

My bodily identity is an illusion and my awareness of love is Reality.

Each time the veil parts, no matter for how long, we get happy for absolutely no reason. These moments are revelatory and bring with it calm, clarity and understanding.

Your inner world expands beyond your ideas.

You may see that your history and conceptual ideas served you and led you to this moment of release. You'll have gratitude for all that you have experienced, even all the pain of suffering when you were so asleep.

Compassion becomes your natural state because you realize the immense gift that life is. And it's not something you worked hard at or earned. It is simply **a gift**.

The dream of suffering had no real effect and was, in fact, meaningless, except to help you choose to get to this moment of release.

We are awakening to this higher state of consciousness and "light reality" with *every* miracle we experience. Our *shifts in perception* **are** the miracles and they are always happening. We are igniting a fire here, as the consciousness shifts.

Although you may not believe the release of fear could be this easy, remember: "Ask not the sparrow how the eagle soars."

There is nothing to fear.

The Fear of Love

It's insane to be afraid of love because love frees you from the dream of separation – entirely.

The love of the Universe is not of your making, it is all powerful and can heal any idea you have that keeps you suffering or in pain. You may not understand how, but just being willing to be shown is all that is required.

The deepest pain, illness and fear is still undone with a simple recognition that you made it up. You can abolish all ideas of sickness, sorrow, and loss. Because you made them up to begin with.

Men have died from the fear of the Love of God, not realizing that they could simply accept it as their reality and go forth to love and serve.

Your ego is not seeing Reality and is utterly confused when confronted with unconditional Love.

It was never you, but the *denial* of who you really are.

Just put it behind you. Its job is to torment you until you are completely free. Resign, surrender, give up all ideas of separation and allow the truth of who you are to be revealed.

You have come for the awakening of the consciousness

and for bringing about a state of peace and harmony on this planet. So be about it. Join with the mighty companions who are beside you on their path. You may not even recognize them yet, but you will.

Your assignment, if you are willing is to accept it, is to do your part in the plan and take no other.

Stay in love and trust that your life is unfolding exactly as it should.

Questions to think about...

Do you experience an inner voice? A knowing? A feeling of being helped?

Do you trust that voice or knowing?

When you listen to that voice, do you feel better or worse?

Does the voice challenge you or bring you insights to your problems?

CHAPTER 11

FREEDOM

Are you struggling with your circumstances and think something is missing? Do you feel that something is terribly wrong, and you can't find it to fix it?

Maybe you think it's you.

When we experience disappointment, like divorce or loss of a loved one, we are challenged to see it from a higher perspective. Loss can cause deep resentment and unhealed pain. When life doesn't work out the way we want, we begin to question what it's all about.

Add to this the demands of taking care of an elderly parent, or children who are addicted or in pain themselves. We often feel cheated, as our lives sometimes unravel before us, and we experience loss and financial insecurity.

For women especially, a sudden divorce, a diagnosis, or loss of custody can cause intense fear. Fear of surviving the ordeal and fear of the unknown.

Often it means it's time for these patterns to come to the surface. We just didn't know how to face these fears before.

Now, they finally catch up with us. We often wonder how we could have denied our own feelings for so long.

If we let go of trying to fix it, we *can* change.

And then life will open up to a new vista. We may *finally* begin to look within and ask the important questions.

Why am I here? What's the purpose of my life? How can I help?

It takes work, dedication, and persistence to get through these challenging periods and come to discover who you are and what you really want to do next.

Finding Meaning in the Mundane

We need to give ourselves permission to be free just to be ourselves and live life as we choose.

We are not often rewarded for the most important accomplishments in life—like raising a child. It's an enormous achievement! But *without acknowledgment*, we don't feel it. Worse, we judge ourselves by how our kids turned out. We wrongly associate *our worth* with their well-being and we judge ourselves for all we did wrong.

Being present and acknowledging yourself is its own

reward. Your life is already a gift. It doesn't have to be anything beyond what it already is.

Our lives don't have to have some grand purpose other than doing simple tasks *with love.* Giving of ourselves can be small or large, and neither size nor the impact matters.

Life can really be that simple. Being at peace with yourself is a rare accomplishment. And it has effects we may not even see.

Appreciation for the simplest encounters is key. A walk in nature. Breathing. Meditation. A vulnerable conversation. A healing talk. Making a meal for someone. Stopping. Slowing down. Silence. Listening.

We can always choose to give of ourselves by doing the simplest of things for others. But put yourself in the mix of those you give to. It's important to take the time for you, too.

Love is the answer. Find the place within us where the love resides, where we connect with ourselves and others – and then offer help. Connection to me is critical to my emotional well-being. I struggle when I think my life is all about me.

It's time to open up, reach out and connect to others if you're always focusing on you. How can you give? How can you make one other person feel loved today?

I am happiest when I'm just being myself, playing music, writing, coaching, healing, teaching, meeting new people and joining with them. I frequently reach out to someone to just see how they're doing.

I'm not a body, I'm free. This is repeated over and over in *The Course*. Free isn't objective. It's a state of mind.

Coming Out of Isolation

When I was a stay at home mother with two small boys, I often felt isolated from others. I thought there was something wrong with me. I didn't find it joyful, but often boring, repetitive and lonely. I couldn't resolve my struggle with the tediousness of my life.

I didn't understand how people found motherhood so fulfilling, when I suffered and didn't want to face the same tasks every day. I loved my kids, but the loneliness was palpable.

I began to *accept* that I wasn't like other people.

My mentors explained that we are all on different time-lines. We are choosing what we want life to mean every single moment.

So comparison with others doesn't work.

My life is about finding a way out of limitation. So I had

to experience a lot of it to ask for help. I didn't know that was what was happening, I just knew I wasn't really happy with a normal human existence. It just wasn't enough. I wanted to be free.

Being a mother taught me patience. Infinite patience.

To trust in the moment and not try to fix it or make it something else, was really challenging for me.

When I was in distress, I tried to rush through my day and do it perfectly, trying to make it all work out for my husband and the kids.

I discovered that I had another purpose for my life; and while at home with the boys, I was experiencing and exploring my spiritual connection and healing.

In hindsight, my kids taught me some of the most important lessons of all, such as: how to be present, how to show up for someone else with grace, how to love and discipline without getting angry and losing my temper. (That took a while!)

Most importantly, how to let them go, when they went to pre-school and then to let them go altogether when it was time. I often had no idea what to do with myself when I did get time to myself. It was weird how I longed for alone time, but then didn't know how to enjoy it.

Once the boys went to live with their father, I had a completely different life. It was a major part of my spiritual practice to let this situation teach me to how to love them from a distance.

I worked full time as a server in a restaurant and saw them on all their school vacations and a month in the summer. We did have a very close relationship after that, but it was so strange to have such limited contact with them. I had a gaping wound in my heart from this for years, and it took a long time to be completely healed.

I had a lot of guilt and hurt about what had happened in the custody trial. It made no sense to me. I had no control over the outcome of that situation, but I learned an important lesson. Here it is.

True Love is Letting Go

Love is not something we can possess, it is freely given and freely received. When we attempt to exchange love, it is imprisoning and binding.

Possession is *not* love. Making someone adhere to your wishes is not love. It's trying to get someone to fit into your dream according to how you see it.

The teaching that has helped me the most is this: The way

to protect everything you love is by the act of giving it away. In other words, what you bind on Earth is bound in Heaven.

"I will give you the keys of the kingdom of heaven; whatever you bind on earth will be bound in heaven, and whatever you loose on earth will be loosed in heaven." Matthew 16:19 NIV

Letting the people in your life be who they are – without your needs placed upon them is liberating – for *all* of you.

Setting each other free from expectations is easier than you think. You will discover real freedom and love by choosing acceptance. Self-love cannot be threatened by other people and their thoughts and beliefs.

People come and go all the time into and out of our lives.

Is it painful? If so, look at what *you believe* about what should happen.

When you have an expectation that people won't ever leave you, you are setting yourself up for pain. They will eventually leave you, but that *doesn't* mean they don't love you.

LOVE IS.

When I realized my love for my kids had nothing to do with how often I saw them, I was set free! We are connected eternally and nothing can separate us in Reality.

That's how love is, it never ends.

I choose to love each of my husbands just as much as when we were together. They don't have to know about it. It's a choice to extend love and forgiveness and let go of resentment.

It's natural to love people whom you struggled with in life. They taught you the most powerful lessons. That's real love, especially when you separate and you find yourself having to start over. It's where the rubber meets the road.

Can your situation teach you how to love yourself more, especially during heartbreak?

Denying yourself love is often the root cause of all your suffering. Can you forgive yourself for learning to love yourself through loss?

Sometimes we don't realize how much we abandon ourselves because of our fear of being alone.

Yet, our soul never feels alone. It's in a state of wholeness and communication with all of life.

Fear of being alone is one of the deepest fears that drives our lives and when we cling to it, we suffer.

Finding Inner Freedom

Do you feel comfortable being alone? Do you know that you are complete and whole within yourself?

Maybe your purpose is simply to find that you can be OK on your own.

A lot of us are single in the later years of our lives and it can be difficult to accept. Pay attention to your fear of being alone. Let it teach you something.

Can you really be alone? Ask yourself that question and get to the bottom of what you're really afraid of, underneath it. There are 7.8 billion people here. Really. Is it possible to be alone? Isn't that just a thought…a lie?

My fear of being alone was a big one. I had to finally give in to living alone when I turned 60 and learn what it means to be comfortable in my own company.

It took something. I had a lot of anxiety come up and couldn't understand why. I value community and connection and I had moved to a new state.

Love is freedom from fear, freedom from bondage to ideas of "not enough", "all alone", "abandoned".

These are all lies we tell ourselves. Taking the time to meditate, do the inner work will help you move beyond your fear. I hope you will practice one of the methods included in this book to do the inner work to undo these beliefs that keep you in pain.

What really worked was making videos on Facebook and reaching out to others. I figured I wasn't the only one feeling this way. Especially when COVID hit. I had just moved to Orlando and suddenly realized, I had to stay home. My ideas of connecting with new friends and a community suddenly dried up.

These times challenge us in the deepest ways. Then, I got serious about what I'm doing here. I kept on connecting and offering my programs online. I got serious about completing this book. I took on my life purpose and found ways to reach out to people online.

Purpose

When you find your life purpose, it is usually something you are drawn to do from within your soul. It's often something you have experienced and overcome, and can offer someone else support with as they go through it.

When you have compassion for people in pain, you may have an intense need to extend healing you received. It frees you.

Sharing your healing with others is where the miracles happen. Your calling or purpose could be solving an issue that you care deeply about because you have experienced it.

When you take the time to explore what you feel, how it makes you happy to be of service in some way – it means that you have their best interest at heart. You want *them* to be happy, so you dedicate your life to helping *them* find their solution.

When you have found your own direct contact with your Higher Self, you become more sensitive to other people's pain. You recognize their pain is your pain.

Joining with people to offer help with no expectations and no defenses can be a life changing experience. We need to share our healing with others to recognize our oneness.

The plan is that when we are in need, someone who has been there can help you. Then you can turn around and help someone else. That's how the 12 Step Program works as well as many other successful transformation programs that have affected millions of people.

Spending Time in Quiet

We can open up to receiving more love and extending it at any given moment. Cultivating self-love opens us up to give more of ourselves, to learn that giving and receiving are really the same thing.

Getting in touch with our feelings of loss and separation creates self-acceptance. We learn how to pay attention to what we need, what we feel we are missing. That way, we cultivate self-love.

I often feel that what I'm learning about myself is so much more important than my circumstances. In fact, adversity is a great teacher.

I don't always know *how*, but I feel blessed and know that by opening up and receiving others, I can listen, stay open to what's needed, simply by being present.

I challenge people to look within themselves, to *discover* their real Self, and their unique gifts they want to give the world. I know it's deep work, and it will transform your life. It's completely worth it.

YOU are what you have been seeking. Self-realization is the "pearl worth any price".

Questions to think about…

How do you feel when you are completely alone?

What problem have you solved in your life that could be of benefit to others?

Can you trust in your compassion for others to guide you?

CHAPTER 12

MENTORING IN THE AGE OF ENLIGHTENMENT

The Self is our teacher as we grow and learn through experiencing our lives. Theories, concepts, and intellect are needed along the way. Yet, all this, including our intellect, is often a barrier to love.

We don't know the unknown until we challenge our beliefs and conditioned reactions to situations. We don't have all the answers. We aren't supposed to. There are many Masters who have conquered the ego, and they all say the same thing. Stop trying to figure it out and pretend that you know.

There's a much bigger picture going on here. It's not of your making...even the world you see is projected from your visual cortex of your brain.

The world we see denies the light of spiritual sight and higher vibration. And we need help to get beyond our own limited understanding.

In the Eastern tradition, it's called ignorance. In *A Course in Miracles*, it's called a dream or illusion. To truly master yourself and come into your Highest Self, you will need some support.

Teachers have the privilege of serving people. No matter where you are on your journey, someone has traveled that road before you and knows the way.

I have had spiritual teachers or mentors for years beginning in 1989. My teachers and guides helped me come out of the darkness of my own denial, and learn how to release my fear.

I've also had the extreme good fortune to have been in the circle of an extraordinary Master Teacher from 1999 to 2008 at the Endeavor Academy in Wisconsin. He demonstrated daily an inexhaustible love, joy, and light.

Day after day, for more than 20 years, he taught *A Course in Miracles*, Bible class on Sundays, quantum physics, stem cell research, universal time travel, parallel universes and much more. He was totally dedicated to showing us the way out of time. His mind was completely different from human minds.

When I was with the Master Teacher, I was always amazed at his energy. The moment I met him, I burst out laughing...for no reason whatsoever! He would travel across the world and come back and be on fire the next day to teach, heal and wake us up.

He took our calls for help, made us laugh with exuberant joy each time we came together. When there were very difficult moments of conflict in my life, I could call him on the phone. He always was available and would pick up and talk to me and reassure me that my problem was already solved.

And he loved music in all its forms, especially jazz. He made over 300 videos. They are all available to everyone worldwide on masterteacher.tv and *A Course in Miracles International* (acimi.com).

While living at the Academy, I was challenged by the intensity of the light, and yet, most of the time I was really happy. I loved being together with other teachers, playing music, singing, dancing, teaching, traveling, and celebrating. We set up centers all over the world.

A big part of our assignment was to disseminate the message of freedom that is *A Course in Miracles*. For a period of seven years, we were involved in litigation to free *A Course in Miracles* from the copyright. It was a long, arduous battle. We were successful, I believe, because this message is too important to be controlled by any one group or person.

Now *The Course* can be published by anyone who chooses to do so. Anyone can find a copy to read and can teach and disseminate the message as they choose. There are many versions and some are online for free (courseinmiracles.com is the Urtext version).

If you are inspired, I encourage you to study it, share it and help one more soul find freedom.

In 2008, the Master Teacher died. I went through a period of grieving and then sorting out what I wanted to do next. I met a man and fell in love. We got married in 2010 and I was really happy. My Dad died in 2013. I kept feeling like I should go back to the East Coast to be closer to my kids and my family. The boys were in college by then and I rarely saw them.

I worked as a massage therapist and Craniosacral therapist in Wisconsin, helping people with both physical pain and trapped emotions. I kept feeling there was something more that I wanted to do, but I didn't know what.

I realized I wasn't serving enough people by working individually. I knew I had a calling to heal the mind. I often coached people while they were on the massage table.

I began to pray for help with *how* to move forward. On New Year's eve in my office with a small group, I heard myself say that I wanted to impact more people.

Within four months, my third husband announced that he wanted out of our marriage. I was *shocked* and *angry*. I went for a jog, asked where I should go, and someone came toward me with a sweatshirt with the word MAINE in large letters. I've learned to follow these signs.

Three weeks later, I left Wisconsin and drove to Maine, my home state, to start my life over again.

My sister welcomed me with open arms and my brothers offered me much needed support and help. I lived with my eldest brother for the summer to get on my feet and see where I wanted to go from there.

Lisa Natoli and Bill Free had started The ***Teachers of God Foundation*** and I *miraculously* ran into her one day at a natural food shop. We had been friends at the Academy. She invited me to her group on Friday morning, so I went. It was awesome to be a part of a community of *A Course in Miracles* teachers once again.

Then, I started following a specific coach online who helps therapists and healers become coaches. She has a Holistic Business School based in Wisconsin. I signed up for her program and a dear friend offered to pay for it for me, and helped me get my start.

I've had so many people here and in spirit to thank for helping me along my journey.

Getting the support I needed, showed me that my life had a purpose. It taught me to *value* my gifts and keep listening to that inner voice.

The Vision

The name **Heal Your Mind Heal Your Life** came to me one day, along with the vision and mission.

Vision:

A world where women are empowered, focused and compassionate leaders and change-makers. We inspire others when we embrace our power and create lives of purpose and commitment to have impact in a positive way.

Mission:

We empower our clients to crush fear, shamelessly love themselves, and change the world by aligning all aspects of their lives. Through education and transformative coaching programs, we achieve our goals.

I set up a website and wrote all the content myself. I began offering retreats and small workshops to help people awaken and find their purpose.

At first, I struggled with charging money. I thought I

wasn't supposed to get paid for a spiritual gift. I had to overcome that idea and recognize it was false.

I was determined to become free of issues with money and self-worth, so I began to offer help to people with money blocks and learned to value my gifts.

I believe money is a way to show we are valued and our work is important– I now help people claim their value and charge what they are worth. It's been a journey of allowing myself to be in service in a way that really works for me.

I struggled with being a leader, being "out there" and on my own. I feel most at ease being the support person and letting others lead. I now embrace leadership as a gift and a responsibility. I've been given so much and I feel it's time to give to people to support them with their growth and well-being.

I'm actually happy being alone, writing or coaching privately. In my childhood, I would always retreat into the privacy of my own room, to write, play music and draw. Yet being part of an orchestra or big band, or a large choir is an extraordinary experience. They both have taught me who I am.

I believe that we each have a unique calling and specific spiritual gifts to give.

We are the way-showers, the heretics who defy the status quo and lead others to find their own purpose, their own voice.

As we embrace our transformation and wake up to who we really are, **we can change our world**.

As we courageously plumb the depths of our denial, we alter our inner *and* outer worlds simultaneously.

We create a new reality of love and light as we go forth to embrace our gifts with open hearts.

Our entire lives become a beautiful gift to the world. And whenever we shine our light, we give permission to everyone else to do the same.

Your gifts are valuable, and I believe spirituality is where *real innovation* comes from.

Life supports us as we awaken. I find that I am taken care of in ways I couldn't even imagine. People have handed me money to help me when I needed it most and new venues have opened up when I wanted to do an event. I'm always given what I need to continue, even when it seems impossible.

Being committed includes being willing to give *and* receive.

> "Our entire lives become a beautiful gift to the world. And whenever we shine our light, we give permission to everyone else to do the same."
>
> ~Monica Dubay

To find your purpose, gives you the means to shine your light and become free to serve those who are drawn to you. Then you are shown how to bring your work into the world by taking certain steps and following your inner guidance.

I am inspired by the courage of people who are willing to create new ideas and innovations. To innovate *change* with *love* ushers in the new paradigm.

The Certainty of Being Yourself

Love is an ever-present Reality, and You ARE THAT. And when you embrace it fully, you have a lot more *power* and *freedom*.

Can you accept yourself exactly as you are right now, with all your idiosyncrasies, faults, memories, judgments, fears, and doubts?

Embracing all that you are makes you a powerful light. And when love and acceptance prevails, everyone wins.

Love doesn't do battle with fear, it simply shines it away.

Don't try to get rid of parts of you that deny the truth. Instead, love them, embrace them with the compassion of a mother for a child, and be released.

You can't get rid of the parts that need love; instead, you need to accept them, even if you don't like this part of you. It's still *you*.

Resistance

If you stay persistent, you will become free because you are the determiner of your reality. You are the Master of your mind and only you can decide what you want to experience.

Your resistance will come up repeatedly. Expect it. It's just a bunch of fear thoughts. Don't let them stop you. Instead, use the methods of release to help undo your fear.

The false self is always resistant, stubborn, attacking, grievous, resentful, and keeps you suffering. So what?

If you want to be a coach/mentor, be sure you have one – because trying to do it on your own is a huge stumbling block. It'll cost you both time and money. And you don't get to serve those people who want to work with you. You are denying them *their* transformation when you give up on yourself.

Fear of change keeps people unnecessarily stuck and in pain *for years*. Don't let this be you.

When I realized I could not get myself out of emotional resistance, I got on my knees and asked for help. My teachers appeared miraculously. I followed my first business coach for a whole painful year before I was ready to get her help. Imagine if I hadn't waited.

We need the reflection from a mentor to move forward and break through resistance. The value of having someone who can help you see where you're stuck is *immeasurable*.

My purpose became clear after I found *A Course in Miracles*. I'm committed to transforming minds. It was a decision I made back in 1989. I've never stopped exploring new ways to bring this about. There's always more to give, more programs, and more people who are seeking support.

Don't you want to help?

Help is always available when you decide you want to embark on your path of growth and self-discovery. Take a chance on it.

I invite you to step into your own light and embrace your journey. People need *you* to lead them.

Leaders are not unafraid, they just don't let fear stop them.

Message: Humanity is shifting in a major way, we are on the brink of a new way of being...are you ready to serve?

Questions to think about...

What mentors/coaches have helped you overcome adversity in your life?

What ways do you resist living with more freedom?

What life lessons have you been through that you could support someone with?

L→R: Monica with her sons Chris and Sam

MONICA DUBAY

Monica Dubay has been a teacher of **A Course in Miracles** since 1989, when she was miraculously healed of anxiety and depression.

Her spiritual training included 12 years with an awakened Master Teacher of **A Course in Miracles** in Wisconsin Dells, Wisconsin.

She is on a mission to help women crush fear, shamelessly love themselves, and change the world. She guides people to discover and embrace their true calling through private and group programs and retreats.

A classical and jazz clarinetist, Monica holds a Master of

Arts in Music from Brooklyn College and a Bachelor of Arts in Music from the University of New Hampshire.

For more support, please visit the website:
www.HealYourMindHealYourLife.com.

Start with the free program, including a workbook and video instruction on "Ten Steps to Create Your Life's Desire".

Digital programs for purchase are included under *Courses*.

For beginners in *A Course in Miracles*, we recommend: The First 50 Lessons of *A Course in Miracles*, including 36 video instructions.

HEAL YOUR MIND HEAL YOUR LIFE

Vision

A world where people are empowered, focused and compassionate leaders and change-makers. We inspire others when we embrace our power and create lives of purpose and commitment to have impact in a positive way.

Mission

We empower women to crush fear, shamelessly love themselves, and change the world by aligning all aspects of their lives. Through education and transformative programs, we achieve our goals.

PLEASE RATE MY BOOK

I would be honored if you would take a few moments to rate my book on Amazon.com.

Or, if you're in any of these countries, please use these Amazon sites:

Amazon.ca (Canada)

Amazon.co.uk (U.K.)

Amazon.com.au (Australia)

Amazon.fr (France)

Amazon.de (Germany)

Amazon.co.jp (Japan)

Amazon.com.mx (Mexico)

Amazon.es (Spain)

A five-star rating and a short review ("Excellent resource!" or "You can experience real transformation. Get this book!") would be much appreciated. I welcome longer, positive comments as well.

If you feel like this book should be rated at three stars or fewer, please hold off posting your comments on Amazon.

Instead, please send your feedback directly to me, so that I can use it to improve the next edition. I'm committed to providing the best value to my clients and readers, and your thoughts can make that possible.

You may reach me at <u>healyourmindnow@gmail.com</u>.

Thank you,

Monica

Author, Transformation Leader
Spiritual Guide, Speaker, Healer
Founder of The Mindset Mastery Method
Publisher, Monica Dubay Publications